THE BEST DEFENSE?

A REPORT OF THE STANFORD UNIVERSITY TASK FORCE ON PREVENTIVE FORCE
Chairmen: Hon. George P. Shultz, Hoover Institution and
Coit D. Blacker, Freeman Spogli Institute for International Studies

THE BEST DEFENSE?

Legitimacy and Preventive Force

by
Abraham D. Sofaer

HOOVER INSTITUTION PRESS

Stanford University   Stanford, California

Hoover Institution Press Publication No. 576

Hoover Institution at Leland Stanford Junior University, Stanford, California, 94305-6010

First printing 2010

16 15 14 13 12 11 10   9 8 7 6 5 4 3 2 1

Manufactured in the United States of America

The paper used in this publication meets the minimum Requirements of the American National Standard for Information Sciences—Permanence of Paper for Printed Library Materials, ANSI/NISO Z39.48-1992.

Cataloging-in-Publication Data is available from the Library of Congress.

ISBN 978-0-8179-1004-4 (cloth : alk. paper)
ISBN 978-0-8179-1005-1 (pbk. : alk. paper)
ISBN 978-0-8179-1003-7 (e-book)

Contents

Foreword:
An Ounce of Prevention Is
Worth a Pound of Cure

Old sayings often contain wisdom. I like the one that says, "An ounce of prevention is worth a pound of cure." Actually, I think it should be quite a few pounds of cure.

Prevention can take many forms. No doubt the most important, from the standpoint of the topic of this report, is learning how to prevent the need to use preventive force. We gave this issue a great deal of thought during our deliberations in the Task Force on Preventive Force. Every member of our group at Stanford, as well as all the scholars, diplomats, and national security experts we met during the three years of work on this project, agreed on the importance of avoiding the use of preventive force whenever possible.

Special attention must be given to those aspects of international security that are the source of our greatest fears, and that thereby generate the greatest pressure on leaders to act preventively. The most important example of such a threat is the possible use of nuclear weapons. The threat of nuclear weapons must be addressed and reduced systematically. The more states that have these weapons, the more fragile will be the application of deterrence strategy as a way of preventing their use. Of course, the terrorists who now seek nuclear weapons essentially cannot be deterred. If they get a weapon, they will use it.

We will progress in reducing the threat of the use of nuclear weapons, and other major threats that might lead to the use of preventive force, only if we develop our capacity to evaluate these complex problems, develop workable solutions to them, and then implement those solutions effectively. Nothing significant can be done to address the problem of, and eventually eliminate, nuclear weapons—or any other major source of international insecurity—without effective diplomacy. Intense and persistent diplomacy is needed, for example, to implement the steps that have been identified as the road to a world safe from nuclear weapons. Diplomatic leadership from the very top is essential. But successful diplomacy needs the presence of strength and the will to use it when necessary.

Anyone who has seen combat is especially careful in suggesting the use of force. But even with the best of efforts to avoid using preventive force, circumstances will arise when difficult decisions about its use must be confronted.

When I was in office (and long before and long after), the United States and our friends were attacked repeatedly. Remember the Israeli athletes at the Olympics in Munich, Sadat's assassination, the Marine barracks bombing in Beirut, the bombing of various embassies, the USS *Cole*, the World Trade Center, and more. Our responses were mild, and the prevailing notion was that these acts of terror presented a problem for law enforcement: catch the people responsible, try them, and, if guilty, put them in jail.

With the attack of 9/11, this thinking changed. The consequences of an act of terror were seen, in fact, to be huge in human and other terms, and would be potentially even more disastrous were weapons of mass destruction to fall into the hands of terrorists. The conclusion was practically a no-brainer; if you can stop the act from happening, you are infinitely better off. So the underlying doctrine of prevention and the possibility of the use of preventive force emerged.

Every terrorist act takes place somewhere: Jakarta, Riyadh, New York, Istanbul, Bali, Washington, D.C., London, Madrid, Tokyo, and so on. What follows, of course, is the urgent importance of local effort to prevent these assaults. We have seen stepped-up efforts everywhere to find out about terrorist plots before they occur and to stop them. Many successes have been achieved.

These stepped-up efforts obviously put great emphasis on intelligence and, since many of the plots originate in other countries, the need for states to share intelligence is clear. This is tricky business because of the absolute need to protect sources and methods. Beyond that, the country that is the target may have a different and more urgent view of when to act than the country providing the intelligence. The country that provides intelligence may favor delaying arrests in order to generate more intelligence of greater potential use. The target country is likely to want to act earlier to avoid any risk of harm.

But when the problem for one country stems from what is going on in another, additional issues arise. The use of force by one state within another is a matter of great moment entangled in issues of legality and legitimacy. Let me put forward a few ideas on this subject.

A fundamental aspect of the problem is the question of accountability—the importance of holding people and institutions, public and private, accountable for their actions. Without accountability, without a sense of consequence, a mentality takes over that says, "I can get away with it." That is true whether you are talking about individual behavior or corporate or national reactions to bailouts, acts of genocide, and much more. Here we are talking about the issue of terrorism. So let us look at terrorism through the lens of accountability.

The monstrous acts of Al Qaeda have made the principle of state accountability an established part of the law of nations. After the 1998 bombings of the U.S. embassies in Africa, the Security Council stressed "that every Member State has the duty to refrain from organizing, instigating, assisting or participating in terrorist acts in another State or acquiescing in organized activities within its territory directed towards the commission of such acts...." [Res. 1189] On

December 29, 2000, the Council strongly condemned "the continuing use of the areas of Afghanistan under the control of the Afghan
faction known as Taliban... for the sheltering and training of terrorists and planning of terrorist acts.... [Res. 1333] Then, after September 11, 2001, the Council recognized that the inherent right of
self-defense arose as a result of those attacks, stressing "that those
responsible for aiding, supporting or harboring the perpetrators,
organizers and sponsors of these acts will be held accountable," and
reaffirming that every State is duty-bound to refrain from assisting
terrorists or acquiescing in their activities. [Res. 1368 & 1373]

So, though the use of force is always hazardous, the legal basis
for the principle of state accountability for terrorist attacks is now
clear, and the right of self-defense is acknowledged as an appropriate
basis for its enforcement. Whatever may be the legality, however, it is
also important to establish legitimacy for the use of preventive force.
This will require serious preparatory diplomatic efforts to line up a
coalition of supporting allies who will be there as needed, no matter
what happens, given that preventive actions are inevitably based on
incomplete intelligence and are likely to have unintended, in addition to intended, consequences.

The reality is that reliable intelligence about impending threats
from shadowy groups is hard to obtain. So the world is seldom black
or white but is more often grey or polka dotted. Probing questions
are always in order. In the end, policy makers have to make difficult
judgments.

If you know about an impending threat, take action, and then
discover that the intelligence about the threat was faulty (no weapons of mass destruction in Iraq), you pay a price—sometimes a large
one. If you know about an impending threat and decide to wait for
more information or dismiss its importance (failure to connect the
dots before 9/11), and then an act of catastrophic dimensions occurs,
you've made a mistake of even greater proportions. So the subject of
the use of preventive force is tough terrain for policy makers.

We have a lot to lose if we fail to strike a proper balance on this issue. A world once split by the cold war now operates as a global economy, able to raise standards of living by a broader application of the law of comparative advantage. Low-income-per-capita countries, as in the case of China, India, Brazil, now Indonesia, and others, are experiencing rapid economic advances. New middle classes are emerging. Poverty, while still a huge problem, has been declining, and that trend will likely persist. Of course, there are plenty of problems. But the world has never been at such a propitious moment—an age of opportunity is ours.

This book consists of an analysis of the problems, as identified by our Task Force, and as ably and clearly described by the author. It represents the best judgments of the Task Force on the dangers of using preventive force, the widespread and perhaps growing practice of doing so, and the absence of workable legal norms for guidance. Our proposed solution, regardless of one's view of the legal issues, is to focus intensely and in a concrete, standard-oriented way, on the legitimacy of such actions. Legitimacy is not an easy concept to apply, but, as spelled out in this study, it is meaningful and practical, with standards based on the likely reactions of the relevant and responsible international community.

No state can avoid its responsibility to the United Nations Charter, or to its own people, by simply invoking legal rulings or pronouncements that are unlikely to stand the test of time. We have to look to the Charter's purposes, and to our own national constitutions, for guidance on issues that are likely to determine the future of civilization. A clear and deep understanding of the relevant concerns is more likely than anything else to help decision-makers reach sound results. This report provides that understanding.

George P. Shultz
Hoover Institution
Stanford University

Acknowledgments

This project continues the constructive cooperation among branches of the Stanford University/national security family. The task force is grateful to each division that supported the project monetarily or by encouraging personnel to cooperate or both. The Hoover Institution and the Freeman Spogli Institute for International Studies bore the brunt of the cost at the university, but our major partner was the William and Flora Hewlett Foundation, the executive director of which, Paul Brest, agreed to serve on the task force as well. With Hewlett's support, the task force was able to hold conferences abroad, which we believed would be critical in demonstrating our interest in the positions of foreign states and from which we learned a great deal on every level of exchange. The foreign meetings could also not have been possible without the support of the Rockefeller Foundation, which contributed its conference center in Bellagio, Italy; the Fuji Xerox Company, which made possible the use of the conference center at Gotenba, Japan; and All Nippon Airways, which contributed support. Finally, the Koret Foundation made contributions to enable the task force to publish this study. Expressions of thanks to the many individuals who helped put the meetings together, or who did research, are contained in the book itself, to the extent feasible.

CHAPTER ONE

Introduction

$\mathcal{G}$rave new threats to peace and security have led to increased efforts at the national and international level to prevent the harm these threats can cause. While punishing perpetrators and assisting victims after the fact is essential and may deter attacks, the highest level of protection comes from actually preventing harm. Terrorist attacks, including those of September 11, 2001, on the United States and subsequent attacks in Asia and Europe, have killed or injured thousands and caused grave social and economic disruption. States have also inflicted massive deprivations of human rights on their own populations. While these acts are illegal under established principles of international law, States are often unable or unwilling to prevent or punish these violations, and sometimes cause or seek to exploit such conduct. The possible acquisition of weapons of mass destruction (WMD) greatly enhances the threats posed by terrorist groups and irresponsible States.

The value of preventing harm is universally recognized, whether it involves keeping a disease from spreading, forestalling violent crime, or heading off terrorist attacks or even genocide. States routinely deal preventively with the threat of domestic terrorist attacks, human rights violations, and other criminal activities. States also cooperate with each other in implementing preventive strategies.

And prevention is the natural objective of military measures taken during armed conflict. While the use of preventive force in these contexts raises issues as to its proper scope and implementation, States in general have broad authority to take reasonable and necessary preventive steps.

States are far more constrained, however, in the non-consensual, international use of preventive force. The United Nations Charter gives the Security Council authority to determine when threats to international peace and security exist, and to authorize the use of force in response to such threats, including threats from terrorism, WMD, and violations of human rights. When the Charter was written, the Council was expected to have at its disposal the armed forces necessary to implement its decisions and thereby to prevent the harm such threats have caused in human history.[1] Based in part on this expectation, the Charter limits the power of individual States to use force in exercising their "inherent" right to defend themselves against armed attacks, or to act collectively in doing so. This authority enables States to use preventive force only when an armed attack against them is underway or so imminent as to preclude resort to the Council for assistance. But the Council, forced to rely on ad hoc contributions of troops from its member States and crippled by disagreements among its permanent members, has been unable to play its intended role. States have therefore been left to deal unilaterally or in alliances with threats that differ from the conventional armed attacks contemplated in the Charter. In responding to the dangers posed by these unconventional threats, States have resorted to a range of preventive actions within the sovereign territories of other States. The propriety of such actions has justifiably become a matter of widespread concern.

The need to respond to international threats through force varies with the potential consequences of the perceived threat and the likelihood of its realization. Some current threats are widely regarded as posing substantial danger, and efforts have been underway for many years, nationally and internationally, to prevent them from being realized. Whether these efforts should include the use of force depends not only on the potential benefits of preventive actions (i.e., the potential harm avoided), but also on potential consequences and costs. Even preventive medicine, despite its benefits, at some point becomes infeasible or undesirable due to adverse consequences and expense.

The use of anticipatory force in international security affairs, including "preventive force," became a matter of heightened interest with the issuance of the 2002 National Security Strategy for the United States (2002NSS). The 2002NSS stated that the United States, despite its unrivaled power relative to other States, faces grave and unprecedented threats that require greater reliance on preventive force.[2] Relying solely on defensive measures, the report concluded, was no longer an effective plan for U.S. security, due to the nature of unconventional attacks and the capacity and willingness of States and non-state actors to target noncombatants. The increasing potential for such States and non-state actors to obtain WMD makes the threat particularly strong.

The 2006 National Security Strategy (2006NSS) reaffirmed these conclusions. It cited four steps it considers necessary for "short term" U.S. security (page 12):

- Prevent attacks by terrorist networks before they occur.
- Deny WMD to rogue states and to terrorist allies who would use them without hesitation.
- Deny terrorist groups the support and sanctuary of rogue states.
- Deny terrorists control of any nation for use as a base and launching pad for terror.

The decision by the U.S. government to make possible use of preventive force an explicit aspect of its national security plan drew widespread debate as to its effectiveness, legality, and legitimacy. The United States had considered and rejected using preventive force during the Cold War, navigating through that period without a major conflict with the Soviet Union or China. The United States' definition of the concept of self-defense (based on "reasonableness") is less constraining than the view of the International Court of Justice (ICJ), which requires an actual or imminent "attack" before using force. It has also at times advocated and used "active measures" in response to terrorist attacks, rather than relying exclusively on criminal investigation and prosecution for deterrence.[3] But the United States had not previously suggested that force may be used to prevent attacks that are anticipated, but neither imminent nor part of an already established pattern of aggression. Also, while the United States has always claimed (and often exercised) the right to use force without Security Council approval when necessary, it subscribes with its NATO allies to the principle that the Council has the primary responsibility for international peace and security. Neither the 2002 nor the 2006 National Security Strategy, however, mentions the Security Council's role.

The 2002NSS and 2006NSS generated considerable criticism and concern. But the premise that prevention must be the primary objective of national and international security strategy in dealing with contemporary threats has widespread support. The seriousness of the threat posed by extremist groups and irresponsible regimes was demonstrated by Al Qaeda's repeated attacks: on the World Trade Center (1993), U.S. embassies in Africa (1998), the USS *Cole* in Yemen (2000), and the World Trade Center and Pentagon (2001). By 2001, Al Qaeda had become a worldwide presence, sponsored by the Taliban regime in Afghanistan and supported by other States and Islamic groups, despite its leaders' avowed objectives and their interest in acquiring and using WMD. Since then, the Taliban regime has been removed from power, but Taliban resistance continues in Afghanistan through suicide bombings and other forms of terrorism. The Taliban also controls areas of both Afghanistan and Pakistan.

Moreover, Al Qaeda and its supporters have been able to attack civilians in Indonesia (2002), Morocco (2003), Spain (2004), and England (2005), killing almost 500 people and injuring many more. Al Qaeda in Iraq participated actively in an insurgency that has killed or injured many thousands of civilians, along with Iraqi and U.S. forces, and disrupted political and economic progress. Iran and Syria actively support Hezbollah in Lebanon and Hamas in Gaza, though both groups have attacked Israel indiscriminately. Finally, grave human rights violations have taken place in several States in recent years, without effective preventive actions by the international community or individual States.

The importance of these issues led scholars at Stanford University to form a study group to evaluate legal and policy concerns. The Stanford Task Force on Preventive Force met periodically during 2005 and 2006 with experts in relevant fields to consider the need for, and implications of, increased reliance on preventive force. The meetings were chaired by former Secretary of State George P. Shultz, the Thomas W. and Susan B. Ford Distinguished Senior Fellow at the Hoover Institution, and Dr. Coit D. Blacker, director of Stanford's Freeman Spogli Institute for International Studies, and with the sponsorship of the Hewlett Foundation.[4]

The Task Force recognized from the outset that a State considering force in response to a security threat must first exhaust the full range of alternatives. Both the 2002NSS and 2006NSS discuss measures short of force, as do many other studies, including the *Report of the High-level Panel on Threats, Challenges and Change* (High-level Panel report),[5] and individual studies such as Ashton B. Carter and William J. Perry's *Preventive Defense* (Brookings 1999). The 2006NSS states, in summarizing the 2002 position (page 18): "Our preference is that nonmilitary actions succeed." The Task Force agrees that, before resorting to any use of force, a State should utilize fully and creatively all available measures to deal with security challenges. This position was consistently stressed and universally supported in discussions held by the Task Force with other U.S. and foreign national security practitioners and scholars.[6]

Where preventive measures short of force fail to resolve security threats, however, resort to force may be the only viable option. The Task Force has therefore considered the propriety of using force when necessary to prevent certain types of anticipated attacks, even though they may not be "imminent," and even without Security Council approval.[7] These issues have generated significant debate among governments, national security professionals, and scholars throughout the world.

After an internal review, the Task Force prepared a written analysis to facilitate discussions with other practitioners and scholars, within and outside the United States. These questions were posed at subsequent Task Force meetings:

- Has the world changed in ways that require or permit greater reliance on preventive force, and if so in what ways?
- How does the meaning of "preventive force" differ from "preemption" and other uses of force considered lawful?
- What are the dangers and limitations of relying on preventive force in dealing with security threats?
- To what extent, and for what purposes, do States use preventive force?
- Do alternatives exist to the legal standards traditionally viewed as governing uses of preventive force?
- Is preventive force inherently illegitimate due to unavoidable uncertainties caused by inadequate intelligence?
- When, if ever, would States be justified in using preventive force without Security Council approval?
- What standards and procedures could enhance the legitimacy of preventive force?

An initial version of the Task Force's analysis was considered May 25–27, 2005, at a conference at Stanford University.[8] A second version, revised to reflect comments made then, was considered at a meeting March 15–16, 2006, at the Woodrow Wilson School of Public and International Affairs, Princeton University, chaired by then Dean Anne-Marie Slaughter.[9] That version was further revised for use in discussions with European officials and scholars at a meeting held at the Rockefeller Center in Bellagio, Italy, on June 10–13, 2007,[10] and again for use at a meeting with Asian scholars May 25–28, 2008, in Gotemba, Japan.[11] The draft report was then circulated to African and Latin American practitioners and scholars.[12] Revisions based on the Asia meeting, and on comments from African and Latin American consultations, are incorporated into this Report, now in its final form.

The Task Force hopes that this study provides a practical guide to identifying and considering the issues relevant to preventive uses of force, thereby enhancing the prospect that such uses of force, if undertaken, advance national and international security and the purposes of the United Nations Charter.

CHAPTER TWO

Defining Preventive Force

$\mathcal{T}$he use of force to prevent harm differs in theory and practice from using force to preempt an armed attack. Both are forms of anticipatory force, but the concept of preemptive force is historically associated with response to an armed attack believed to be "imminent" as contrasted with an attack expected at an unknown time. Preemption is widely considered a limited and legally accepted extension of the right of self-defense that has been recognized in international law under Article 51 of the United Nations Charter. Prevention, by contrast, when used in a defensive context, is understood to mean the use of force earlier than the point of "imminence," the point at which preemption is permitted. Prevention may also be undertaken to forestall the realization of threats other than conventional attacks. These definitions summarize the differences:

- To "preempt" is to use force against an attack that is believed to be imminent based on evidence that hostile action has begun or is about to occur.
- To "prevent" is to use force against an anticipated attack based on a judgment that the attacker will use existing or potential means to attack in the future, or to engender other types of harm, including, for example, harm to hostages, attacks by non-state actors, or the mistreatment by a State of its own nationals.

In short, prevention is not just a matter of striking first, before an expected but non-imminent attack, but also any use of force against any threat that does not qualify as an attack or imminent attack under international law.[1]

The distinction between preemption and prevention is important. Preemption strongly implies that an attack is about to occur, thereby establishing a direct relationship between the use of preemptive force and the UN Charter's standard for self-defense. An imminent attack is also more likely to occur than an attack that is merely anticipated. That a threat is non-imminent does not, however, mean that prevention of the hostile action at a time earlier than would be allowed under the doctrine of preemption will necessarily confer fewer benefits or entail greater costs than preempting an imminent attack. The need for applying preventive force will likely depend on considerations other than those that determine the appropriate use of preemptive force.

Justification. Preemptive uses of force are directly related to the U.N. Charter's authorization in Article 51 of the use of force in self-defense "if an armed attack occurs against a Member of the United Nations . . ." Preventive force, on the other hand, has been considered and used historically not only to prevent attacks that are expected though non-imminent, but also to prevent other types of threats, and even to advance a State's self-interest. Preemptive actions are also generally more readily defensible than preventive actions, because it is possible to determine the need for preemptive action with a high degree of confidence through the actions and statements of a hostile actor. The need for preventive action is often (though not always) based on less-certain evidence.

In specific situations, a preemptive action, though legally justifiable, may actually be undertaken to advance the preempting State's self-interest. Preventive action, on the other hand, may be undertaken for unselfish purposes such as saving foreign nationals or domestic populations from serious deprivations of their human rights. Similarly, many threats that States currently face may be more potentially damaging than an armed attack, including terrorist infiltrations and suicide bombings. The evidence supporting preventive actions may also be extremely strong, as in interventions that do not qualify as armed attacks. The international community has recognized as justifiable and within the rubric of self-defense some preventive actions that do not meet the current legal standard to justify a typical action in self-defense.

Likelihood of Attack. An important consideration in contrasting preemptive and preventive force is the likelihood that an anticipated attack will occur if effective action is not taken. Attacks that are imminent would seem, in general, to be more probable actually to occur than attacks anticipated at an indefinite time in the future. Attacks that seem imminent may, however, not actually occur. Furthermore, while non-imminent attacks may, in general, be less likely to occur than imminent attacks, the perceived likelihood of non-imminent attacks will vary substantially, depending, among other things, on the nature and motivation of the threat, the prior conduct and capacity of the State or group from which the attack is anticipated, and evidence of the State's or group's intentions. The more likely a non-imminent attack, the more it may justifiably provoke the high degree of urgency associated with attacks that are imminent. A particularly important consideration is the extent to which the anticipated attacker is believed to be vulnerable to deterrence. It is reasonable to conclude that a State or group prepared to pay any price (including suicide or other seemingly irrational costs) to achieve its objective is more likely to attack a State than a less determined or more rational adversary.

Potential Harm. An important consideration in comparing preemptive with preventive action is the extent of harm an anticipated attack would cause. An attack that is "imminent," though more certain, may be potentially less dangerous than one that is not. The potential cost of delaying some preemptive actions may therefore be less than the potential cost of delaying some preventive actions. In general, the more serious and irreversible the consequences of an anticipated attack, imminent or otherwise, the greater will be the perceived need to act. In some instances, the potential harm from waiting for an attack to become imminent may be significantly greater than if an anticipated attack were to be prevented well before it becomes imminent. For example, an attack on an unfueled nuclear power plant that is perceived to be a source of nuclear weapons material under hostile control may be less costly in lives lost and environmental damage than an attack after fueling and commencement of operations.

Capacity. Another consideration involved in comparing preemptive and preventive force is the real or perceived capacity of the anticipated attacker. An anticipated attack cannot be viewed as imminent before the anticipated attacker is believed to possess the capacity to attack. On the other hand, the capacity to attack immediately does not necessarily establish an imminent threat. Once an anticipated attacker is believed to possess the capacity to launch an immediate attack, however, the situation may fairly be described as "potentially imminent," posing a significantly greater threat than situations in which the anticipated attacker is not yet capable of launching an immediate attack.

Necessity. The definitions of "preemption" and "imminent" are rooted in historical events that make necessity a relevant concern. The historical definition of "imminent"—a need to exercise self-defense that is "instant, overwhelming, and leaving no choice of means, and no moment for deliberation"[2]—implies that insufficient time exists to enlist the assistance of the territorial State. By analogy, the need to act preemptively against attacks cannot exist if sufficient time remains to report the matter to the Security Council in order to permit it to take "measures necessary to maintain international peace and security."[3] This factor suggests a distinction between preemptive and preventive actions that restricts the former to those threats that are so urgent as to preclude notifying the foreign State or Security Council as a potential substitute for unilateral action.

This distinction does not, however, establish that preventive uses of force—in response to non-imminent threats—are always less necessary than preemptive uses of force. Preventive actions are no less necessary than preemptive actions when it is clear that a request to the territorial State or the Security Council would be futile.

CONCLUSION

The distinction between preemptive and preventive uses of force reflects real differences between attacks that are "imminent" and those that are less immediate. Important considerations underlie the distinction between preemptive and preventive uses of force, bearing upon justification, probability, likelihood of harm, and necessity. On the other hand, real-world factors show that using preemptive force isn't always more reasonable or legitimate than using preventive force. The imminence of an attack is an important, but not the only, measure of the need for anticipatory force.

Current Threats and Preventive Force

*S*tates, international and national security officials, and others cite several developments to justify increased reliance on preventive uses of force. This chapter describes those developments and reviews the extent to which international organizations and States regard them as justifying increased reliance on preventive force.

THREATS POTENTIALLY REQUIRING USES OF PREVENTIVE FORCE

Unconventional Threats: Historical standards of law regarding anticipatory force are based on conventional forms of military action, in which regular forces normally mass in preparation for an attack against another State. The threatened State is potentially able to prepare for and preempt such an attack before it is launched. Conventional attacks still occur. Today, however, the threats of greatest concern include unconventional attacks, which are prepared in secret, launched without warning, and conducted without regard to established rules governing the conduct of war. Instead of using regular forces and conventional military equipment, States or non-state actors use individuals who do not qualify as combatants to attack civilians and non-military targets, such as commercial aircraft, trains, buses, restaurants, and other civilian infrastructure. These attackers attempt to penetrate State borders without being noticed, thereby precluding preemptive action that meets current legal standards. The resulting attacks can be as damaging as conventional ones, while being far more difficult to anticipate.

Failed States and Rogue Regimes: The existence of failed States (whose authority and capacity have eroded to the point that they are incapable of satisfying mandated standards of international conduct) and rogue regimes (which refuse to comply with mandated standards) is often cited as evidence of the increased need to consider using preventive force. International security is based on assumptions related to the powers and responsibilities of States. The U.N. Charter system assumes all States are legally equal and sovereign, and have the power and responsibility to exercise control over security matters within their borders and over their foreign relations. States are obliged to police their territories, to refrain from aggression, to allow no terrorist sanctuaries or training facilities, and to prevent transnational attacks by non-state actors operating from within their territories. They are also required to protect individuals within their territories (whether citizens or not) against grave violations of human rights such as genocide and torture.

States that are unwilling or unable to perform established duties have left areas of the world essentially ungoverned. Some States have used their powers and resources to exploit or support groups prepared to attack other States or their nationals. Others have attacked or allowed attacks on their own nationals based on race, religion, or other discriminatory criteria. In such situations, traditional concepts of sovereignty tend to protect and legitimize incompetent and illegitimate rulers. The principle of State sovereignty retains substantial influence, and significantly constrains the use of preventive force. But evolving norms, especially in the areas of international security and human rights, are undermining the traditional principle that States should have absolute control over what occurs within their borders.

Unprecedented Destructive Capacities: Weapons capable of producing mass casualties or major societal disruption are available, or may soon become available, to increased numbers of States and to non-state actors. The spread of WMD, especially nuclear devices, is perhaps the most widely cited factor relied upon to justify potential resort to preventive force. Membership in the WMD "club" is no longer limited to major States. Current estimates of the States that possess or are developing nuclear, chemical, or biological weapons, and the means of delivery, indicate a trend toward proliferation.

All classes of WMD are capable of creating mass effects, but their dangers vary considerably:

- Nuclear weapons require access to nuclear fuel. This highly enriched uranium or plutonium can only be acquired by production by States running large programs at great expense, or through theft or purchase. Nuclear weapons need considerable technology, access to which can be made more difficult through classification, export controls, and inspection regimes. They are costly and difficult to develop or to replicate in secret, due to the considerable infrastructure required. On the other hand, the gap between acquiring nuclear material on one hand and producing a nuclear bomb on the other is increasingly manageable: nearly half of the enriched plutonium and uranium stores in the former Soviet Union (sufficient to produce 50,000 to 60,000 nuclear weapons) are under inadequate safeguards or accountability. No international agreement exists to control plutonium produced in nuclear reactors.
- Biological and chemical weapons are, or soon will be, widely available to non-state actors. They are relatively inexpensive and can be produced with little or no external footprint. Such weapons can be produced largely (if not entirely) on the basis of knowledge and equipment that is dual-use and widely available. Once developed, they are readily replicated; can be delivered anywhere without great difficulty;

can be used with relatively high confidence that the originator will not be identifiable; and are suited for use against civilian populations (though relatively ineffective on the battlefield). In addition, deterrence is of little use with biological and chemical weapons due to the difficulty of identifying the originator of an attack and the impracticality of responding in kind. Preventing proliferation through international organizations and interstate agreements is also limited by the ability of State and non-state actors to develop them in secret.

Increased Capacities of Non-state Actors: An additional justification for increased reliance on the potential use of preventive force is the claim that non-state actors (including groups using terrorist methods) have acquired significant, unprecedented, transnational capacities resulting from the following circumstances:

- Interconnectedness and openness of modern societies afford transnational actors global mobility and influence.
- Modern communication technologies provide the means for mobilizing and coordinating international efforts of non-state actors.
- Modern weaponry and explosives are obtained, transported, and transferred to and by non-state entities more easily than ever.
- Economic globalization has enhanced the ability of non-state actors to collect and transfer the limited amounts of funding necessary for operations.
- Threats posed by non-state actors are more difficult to detect or control than conventional threats, since non-state actors disregard or exploit legal requirements governing combatants (such as those requiring uniforms and other indicia of combat status) and limits on the use for military purposes of protected institutions (such as schools, hospitals, and religious meeting places).
- Non-state actors appear eager to obtain and use nuclear weapons and other WMD, including "dirty bombs."
- The threat posed by terrorist groups is enhanced by their cooperation with non-state groups engaged in organized criminal activities.

Islamic Radicalism: The threat posed by radical Islamic groups is often cited to justify the possible use of preventive force. Islamic fundamentalist groups with global reach and ambition, acting on the basis of purported religious doctrine, are particularly threatening. Several such groups are well-organized and funded by States and individuals who share their fundamentalist objectives. Not all these groups share all the same objectives, but at least some openly advocate aims that affected States (including some Islamic regimes) are unprepared to accept. For example, Al Qaeda supports removing all Western influence and personnel from the Islamic world, reestablishing an Islamic order in all areas ever controlled by Islam under a restored Caliphate, and destroying the State of Israel. These groups have also demonstrated their willingness to resort to force, including suicidal attacks and mass violence aimed at civilians and using attackers indistinguishable from noncombatants. They seek the most devastating weapons possible and are willing to use them in a manner designed to maximize damage to population centers and economic targets.

Unreliability of Deterrence: Terrorist groups, especially those driven by religious fanaticism, may not be possible to deter. They deliberately engage in suicidal actions, and consider death during *jihad* a desirable outcome. Some have espoused the use of WMD on the assumption that they can cause far more damage to their enemies' morale, population, and wealth than could be inflicted in retaliation. Similar beliefs may exist at the highest levels of some governments. Some political leaders may be prepared to see massive damage inflicted on their countries and nationals in order to achieve what they believe are divinely ordained objectives. Leaders of States may nonetheless be more susceptible to deterrence than non-state actors, since the former are readily identifiable and have permanent locations, while the latter can operate as insurgents with no "return address."

Vulnerability of Democracies: Democratic States are generally target rich countries with vulnerable infrastructures, constrained by legal principles and practices in dealing with threats. While they are technologically advanced, they cannot provide complete security in any significant area of vulnerability. Attacks that have limited physical consequences may nevertheless cause significant short-term and long-term economic harm and lasting psychological insecurity.

POSITIONS OF INTERNATIONAL ORGANIZATIONS
AND STATES ON CURRENT THREATS

These factors are viewed by many international organizations, States, and scholars as significantly altering the nature and level of threats to national and international security. They generally call for increased reliance on preventive measures, though not necessarily on the unilateral use of force.

The United Nations High-level Panel report, for example, concluded that new threats require preventive diplomacy and sometimes require preventive force (page 55):

> In the world of the twenty-first century, the international community does have to be concerned about nightmare scenarios combining terrorists, weapons of mass destruction and irresponsible States, and much more besides, which may conceivably justify the use of force, not just reactively but preventively and before a latent threat becomes imminent.

Similarly, the European Security Strategy lists today's key threats as terrorism, proliferation of WMD, regional conflicts, state failure, and organized crime,[1] stating (page 8):

> Our traditional concept of self-defense—up to and including the cold war—was based on the threat of invasion. With the new threats, the first line of defense will often be abroad. The new threats are dynamic. The risks of proliferation grow over time; left alone, terrorists become ever more dangerous. State failure and organized crime spread if they are neglected as we have seen in West Africa. This implies that we should be ready to act before a crisis occurs. Conflict prevention and threat prevention cannot start too early.

This European evaluation of the security challenge posed by current threats stresses the need for "prevention," but uses the word in a context that leaves ambiguous whether the European Union Strategy supports the use of preventive force to accomplish "conflict prevention and threat prevention."

The United States identifies many of the same developments as requiring consideration of the use of preventive force. It stresses that preventive force is especially necessary to prevent the most dangerous weapons from reaching the hands of the most irresponsible groups.[2]

NATO's position on current threats is aligned with that of the United States and Europe and with the conclusion of the High-level Panel, as reflected in NATO's Strategic Concept and subsequent declarations.[3] NATO declarations support the proposition that current threats justify resort to the full range of preventive measures, including preventive force when necessary. For instance, in October 2003, NATO released its military concept for defense against terrorism, which states that it is based "on the assumption that it is preferable to deter attacks or to prevent their occurrence rather than deal with their consequences and be prepared to deploy as and where required to deal with particular circumstances as they arise."

The positions of European States with regard to the nature and significance of current threats are consistent with those of NATO and the United States. But their positions vary considerably, even among members of NATO, on the extent to which force should be used internationally to prevent these threats. Some expressly disclaim reliance on transnational uses of force as inconsistent with strict international legal limitations.[4]

Asian organizations and States acknowledge the need to deal with contemporary threats to international security, but stress "peace-oriented values" and sovereignty as controlling considerations. The 1976 Treaty of Amity and Cooperation in Southeast Asia emphasizes the peaceful settlement of disputes. It establishes a High Council to "take cognizance" of disputes "likely to disturb regional peace and harmony," but gives it no authority to use force for that purpose.[5] The Charter of the Association of Southeast Asian Nations (ASEAN), adopted in 2007, lists among its purposes, "To maintain and enhance peace, security and stability and further strengthen peace-oriented values in the region," and, most relevant here, "To respond effectively, in accordance with the principle of comprehensive security, to all forms of threats, transnational crimes and transboundary challenges." (Article 1(1) and (8)). The Charter emphasizes, however, the independence and territorial integrity of Member States and the "renunciation of aggression and of the threat or use of force or other actions in any manner inconsistent with international law." (Article 2 (2)). No ASEAN Summit has authorized the use of force. On February 20, 2004, leaders at the Ninth Summit adopted the Bali Concord II stipulating to the establishment of an ASEAN Community resting on "three pillars," including an ASEAN Security Community (ASC). The Plan of Action to implement this policy includes no provision related to the use of force for security or the need to deal with new forms of threats. It does state, however, that "Member Countries shall not condone . . . the use of their territory for any actions undermining peace, security and stability of other ASEAN Member Countries." An Annex includes a section calling for the use of "national peace keeping centers" and indicating an intention to build a regional peacekeeping force, a decision welcomed by the United Nations but opposed by some ASEAN members, including Thailand and Singapore.[6]

Asian attitudes toward the possible use of preventive force were on display after former Prime Minister John Howard of Australia said in an interview on December 1, 2002, that he would act to prevent an attack against Australia being planned in another country: "It stands to reason that if you believed that somebody was going to launch an attack against your country, either of a conventional kind or of a terrorist kind, and you had the capacity to stop it and there was no alternative other than to use that capacity then of course you would have to use it." Howard emphasized that the types of threats faced today differ from conventional wars, and that international law should be adjusted to deal with the new realities:

> [W]hen the United Nations Charter was written the idea of attack was defined by the history that had gone before, and that is that of an army rolling across the border of a neighbouring country, or in the case of the Japanese and Pearl Harbour bombing a base. Now . . . what you're getting is nonstate terrorism, which is just as devastating and potentially even more so. And all I'm saying . . . is that maybe the body of international law has to catch up with that new reality. . . . [A]ny Prime Minister who had a capacity to prevent an attack against his country would be failing the most basic test of office if he didn't utilize that capacity if there's no other alternative.[7]

Several Asian leaders emphatically disagreed with Howard's comments. Prime Minister Mahathir of Malaysia said, for example, that firing a rocket or using an unmanned aircraft to assassinate anybody in Malaysia would be considered a crime and an act of aggression, "and we will take action against the nation which carries out such acts."[8] Spokesmen for Indonesia, Thailand, and the Philippines all announced that using preventive force on their territory would be a breach of their sovereignty.[9] However, not all members of the Asian community absolutely oppose the possible preventive uses of force. A high-ranking Indian official has advanced the view that it "will do whatever it takes" to fight Pakistan-sponsored terrorism in Kashmir, including preemptive operations, noting that India has a "much better case to go for preemptive action against Pakistan than the U.S. has in Iraq."[10]

The Organization of American States (OAS) notes in its October 2003 Declaration on Security in the Americas that "the security threats, concerns, and other challenges in the hemispheric context are of diverse nature and multidimensional scope, and the traditional concept and approach must be expanded to encompass new and nontraditional threats." The Inter-American Convention against Terrorism affirms "the need to adopt effective steps in the inter-American system to prevent, punish, and eliminate terrorism through the broadest cooperation," but focuses on domestic measures such as preventing and eradicating the financing of terrorism, coordinating law enforcement, and providing mutual legal assistance. OAS Charter provisions absolutely prohibit the use of force by any Member State in the territory of another and the Convention on Terrorism adopts no change in that policy.[11]

African States recognize through their regional organizations, the Economic Community of West African States (ECOWAS), the South African Development Community (SADC), and the African Union (AU), that grave threats are currently posed to peace and security in Africa due to human rights violations, especially resulting from the overthrow of democratically elected leaders.[12] ECOWAS intervened in Liberia in 1993 in response to attacks by groups seeking to overthrow its president, Samuel Doe, and its success in that action led its Members to add to its development purpose a commitment to protect human rights and promote democratic systems of government through elections and peacekeeping actions. In 1998, ECOWAS adopted a Framework for conflict prevention and security, creating a Council to authorize military interventions. This was followed in 1999 with a Conflict Protocol that established a mechanism for protecting Member States and authorizing ECOWAS to take enforcement action in response to internal conflicts.[13] In its 2001 Democracy Protocol, ECOWAS made explicit its position that violations of human rights and internal crises are inherently linked to the maintenance of democratic institutions and the rule of law.[14] A similar treaty-making process has expanded the role of SADC, which has since 1993 been engaged in protecting democratic government, human rights, and the rule of law. The SADC Organ on Politics, Defense, and Security assumes responsibility for recommending punitive measures to the heads of state of SADC Members, and was elaborated in a 2004 Conflict Protocol authorizing regional interventions where large-scale conflict or violence exists within a State, a threat exists to the legitimate authority of the government, and to deal with civil war or insurgency, or with any other crisis that threatens the peace and security of Member States.[15]

Many of these measures found their way into the AU governance structure for the African continent. Article 4(j) of the Constitutive Act of the AU, in addition to recognizing the right of Member States to request intervention by the Union to restore "peace and security," provides in Article 4(h) for "the right of the Union to intervene in a Member State pursuant to a decision of the Assembly in respect of grave circumstances, namely: war crimes, genocide, and crimes against humanity."[16] A Protocol, ratified in December 2003, amends Article 4(h) to allow intervention by the Union in respect of "a serious threat to legitimate order to restore peace and stability to the Member State of the Union upon the recommendation of the Peace and Security Council." Simultaneously, the AU established an African Standby Force for the purpose of peace support missions and constitutionally supported interventions. Article 13(3d) of the Protocol Relating to the Establishment of the Peace and Security Council of the African Union allows for "preventive deployment" to keep "(i) a dispute or a conflict from escalating, (ii) an ongoing violent conflict from spreading to neighboring areas or States, and (iii) the resurgence of violence after parties of a conflict have reached an agreement." The Union's Legal Adviser, Ben Kioko, explains that this broad authority to intervene "was born of the inglorious record of massacres, gross and massive violation of human rights, and large population displacements that have made the African continent host to the greatest number of refugees and displaced persons in the world, due to factors ranging from conflicts to bad governance, poverty, failed States and others."[17] While the AU has no treaty provision explicitly aimed at dealing with the threat of terrorism, Alpha Oumai

Konaré, chairperson of the AU Commission, has stated that "international terrorism over the past decade has come to constitute the most serious threat to global peace, security, and development."[18] None of the African regional arrangements authorizing the use of force requires prior approval by the Security Council.

An influential explanation for the African view that force may be appropriate in certain circumstances to prevent irresponsible sovereign conduct was advanced by Ambassador Francis M. Deng of Sudan and others in 1996. Relying on the views of former U.N. Secretary General Boutros Boutros-Ghali, as well as those of former Secretary General of the OAU Salim Ahmed Salim, among others, and reviewing especially the history of conflict in Africa, Ambassador Deng and his coauthors explained that sovereignty entails, not only rights and powers, but also responsibilities, and that the international community should insist on protecting innocent individuals from official misconduct:

> First, sovereignty carries with it responsibilities for the population. It is from acceptance of this responsibility that the legitimacy of a government derives. . . . A government that allows its citizens to suffer in a vacuum of responsibility for moral leadership cannot claim sovereignty in an effort to keep the outside world from stepping in to offer protection and assistance.[19]

CHAPTER FOUR

Categories of Preventive Action

$\mathcal{P}$reventive force is a concept that includes a broad array of possible actions, ranging from limited uses of force to full-scale preventive war.[1] The security, political, and legal considerations associated with preventive actions vary greatly, depending on the category of preventive action contemplated, its context, and the possible consequences of acting or failing to act.

This chapter puts preventive uses of force in context by first examining two areas in which preventive measures are routinely used to deal with threats—national law enforcement and armed conflict—but which are subject to less restrictive requirements than those limiting transnational uses of force. It then reviews the principal categories of the transnational uses of force by States in the post-Charter period in which prevention of harm was claimed to be an objective, as well as the reactions to such uses of preventive force by the Security Council, General Assembly, and other relevant institutions. The practice of States in using force within the territory of other States for preventive purposes provides guidance as to both the perceived need for such actions and why the international community sometimes accepts them despite their failure to meet legal standards.

PREVENTIVE FORCE IN LAW ENFORCEMENT
AND ARMED CONFLICT

Preventive Force in National Law Enforcement

Law enforcement actions involving the use of preventive force, including searches, arrests, detentions, and interrogations, are common within the national territory of States. Such actions are largely governed by domestic rules, such as those in the United States requiring probable cause and limiting force to what is reasonable and necessary. National law enforcement rules differ markedly from international standards governing the use of force. Law enforcement actions permit the use of force, for example, to prevent a planned crime long before it is imminent. Indeed, preventive force is acceptable as soon as probable cause exists that a crime is being planned. A person can be arrested for attempting or conspiring to commit a crime, aiding or abetting other would-be criminals, or providing material support, even if the crime being planned, attempted, or supported never actually takes place.

National law enforcement has long been the principal vehicle for dealing with terrorism in the United States and elsewhere. Many States, in fact, had more extensive experience in dealing with terrorism than the United States before Al Qaeda's attacks. Egypt, England, France, Germany, India, Israel, Italy, Spain, and other states had adopted laws and practices before 2001 intended to increase their ability to investigate, detain, and prosecute terrorists.[2] The United States had some success in preventing terrorist attacks during the 1980s, but controversial investigations and privacy-oriented policies restricted investigative activities and interagency cooperation.[3] After the World Trade Center attack of 1993, the United States began to adopt laws intended to enhance prevention through domestic law enforcement. Still, the United States and other States found their ability to prevent attacks remained limited because of the traditional emphasis on prosecuting rather than preventing criminal activity, and by rules that severely limited intelligence and law enforcement agencies from cooperating and sharing information.[4] Soon after the attacks of September 11, 2001, however, U.S. law enforcement agencies were instructed to give the highest priority to preventing terrorist attacks, broadening the scope for national law enforcement and enhancing interagency cooperation.[5]

This increased emphasis on preventing terrorist attacks has been adopted in many States.[6] Law enforcement measures involving the use of force have been used successfully in several instances in recent years to prevent bombings of airports and other civilian infrastructure.[7] Among the significant attacks that have been prevented through national law enforcement action (at times with international cooperation) are the bombing of aircraft out of Heathrow Airport in London, attacks on British airports, and bombings in Spain by a group captured in Barcelona.[8]

These and other successful preventions of terrorist attacks and security-related crimes are also attributable to new laws and procedures and an increased commitment of resources. Among the types of rules established in recent years are laws and infrastructure to improve control of immigration and to prevent illegal entries. The grounds for entering States have been narrowed in many places, and visa issuance rules have been made more stringent. Surveillance has been authorized with less restrictive standards than in the past, and in the form of far more active and technologically advanced programs. Interrogation has been allowed with fewer restrictions, and has been used more extensively. States have also used their power to define crimes and to use force through investigative and enforcement procedures to prevent those crimes from taking place. New crimes have been created that enable law enforcement to extend these expanded powers into new areas of activity, including, for example, the crime of knowingly assisting a group that supports terrorism.[9] Some States prohibit advocacy for terrorist acts, or have outlawed encouraging radicalism associated with terrorist acts. Financial controls have been imposed on suspect groups, and prohibited transactions have been made criminal. Many States have authorized temporary detention of persons considered dangerous without charge on the basis of prescribed levels of proof and judicial approval.[10] While the United States has not yet adopted a detention law, it has detained individuals on a variety of grounds, including detention pending deportation, as illegal combatants, or as material witnesses.[11]

The wisdom and fairness of some of these policies have been challenged in many States and internationally. Preventive actions in national law enforcement are in principle lawful when authorized by a State within its territory, but they are at times applied in a manner that deprives individuals or groups of civil liberties or their rights against racial and religious discrimination.

The United States and many other States have adopted laws that give their law enforcement officials authority to investigate and capture persons in foreign States for certain crimes against their nationals.[12] International law does not, however, permit States to use their law enforcement powers within the territory of other States. Thus, the implementation of these laws is almost always undertaken through cooperation with the State where enforcement actions occur; without consent, such law enforcement activities violate international as well as the national law of the territorial State. A State may consent to the exercise by another State of law enforcement authority within its borders, and States frequently cooperate in preventing security-related threats, both bilaterally and through international agencies such as the International Police Organization (INTERPOL).[13] The United States has assisted other States, including Pakistan and the Philippines, in capturing or killing terrorist suspects. Yemen permitted the United States to target an individual who both States believed was a member of Al Qaeda and among the perpetrators of the attack on the USS *Cole* in 2000.[14] States may also agree by treaty or on an ad hoc basis to assist each other in capturing or killing suspected criminals, including members of terrorist groups. Such cooperative arrangements are widespread, and often reciprocal. Extradition treaties, for example, usually provide for the arrest and removal to the requesting State of any person who has been properly accused in the requesting State of a crime listed in the treaty as warranting such cooperation. Also, States often cooperate informally with other States by turning over individuals suspected of committing or planning to commit crimes, usually non-nationals. This practice, termed "rendition," is much more often used than formal extradition.[15] In recent years, renditions have been used to move individuals to States in which they are interrogated, sometimes tortured, with no formal charge or hearing. This practice has been challenged under both national and international legal principles.[16]

Additionally, under certain circumstances, States may use law enforcement measures in international waters. For example, a State may enforce its national law on vessels that fail to fly the flag of any State, or where reasonable grounds exist to believe that the vessel is being used to ship contraband.[17] This principle of "reasonable grounds" led to the interception of the vessel BBC *China* in international waters, exposing the A.Q. Khan nuclear black-market network.[18] In September 1987, U.S. law enforcement personnel implemented a plan that enticed Fawaz Yunis, one of the hijackers of a Royal Jordanian airliner in 1985, onto a vessel in Cyprus that took him into international waters where he was arrested and transported to the United States for prosecution.[19] International law has in addition long recognized the right of any State to seize or attack pirates in international waters; they have been regarded as international outlaws.[20] State action is permitted and sometimes required by the Maritime Terrorism Convention to prevent, capture, prosecute, or extradite persons who have made attacks on private vessels.[21]

The United States relied on established law and practice in fashioning the Proliferation Security Initiative (PSI), under which more than ninety States have agreed to interdict vehicles, planes, or vessels believed to be engaged in the illegal proliferation of weapons and technology.[22] The PSI does not include a provision contemplating resort to the Security Council for prior approval, since the actions its parties agree to take are based on established domestic and international legal authority. The Council has implicitly approved such interdictions in Resolution 1540, which "decided that all States shall refrain from providing any form of support to non-state actors" attempting to obtain or use weapons of mass destruction, and shall "take and enforce effective measures to prevent the proliferation" of WMD.

International law does limit the exercise of domestic law enforcement powers in certain respects. Most States have ratified and incorporated into their laws certain conventions that govern State conduct, in particular the Conventions against Genocide and Torture and the Geneva Conventions governing the treatment of prisoners. Other, universally accepted principles of international law may also limit State authority, such as the prohibition of racial discrimination in the infliction of serious punishments. These limits apply regardless of claimed emergencies, and indeed are designed to prevent States from invoking alleged or actual emergencies as justification for proscribed conduct.[23]

Despite increased recognition by law enforcement officials of the need to give priority to prevention in security-related investigations, long-entrenched practices are difficult to overcome. Investigative agencies and prosecutors continue to give significant weight to obtaining evidence usable at trials, and to allowing investigations to proceed to the point that a prosecution will be successful. States that share a strong commitment to prevention may undermine their ability to prosecute suspects by adhering to limits on the admissibility of evidence at trials.[24] Successful prevention is also hindered by the continued failure of governments and agencies to share intelligence. Sharing information is unwise when it could lead to security breaches but, in general, cooperation among agencies and between trusted States increases effective detection.[25] Finally, some States simply refuse to cooperate in security-related investigations and prosecutions aimed at preventing terrorist actions. In such cases, threatened States lack authority under existing standards of international law to act within the territories of the non-cooperating States. As discussed below, however, States sometimes unilaterally engage in preventive actions within those territories.

Preventive Force in Armed Conflict

Combatants in an armed conflict are allowed to use necessary and proportionate force, including anticipatory force, against the enemy.[26] Every use of force in armed conflict must comply with the laws of war, but no separate justification for using anticipatory force is required in such situations.

Based on this principle, the attacks perpetrated by Al Qaeda, before and on September 11, 2001, provided ample justification, in the view of most international lawyers, for the United States to use force against Al Qaeda and its members within Afghanistan and against its sponsoring regime, the Taliban, regardless of whether an additional attack was imminent.[27] The UN Security Council affirmed this position when it unanimously resolved that the attacks of September 11, 2001, justified the use of force by the United States in self-defense under Article 51 of the UN Charter.[28] Al Qaeda leaders not only claimed responsibility for the September 11 attacks, they announced their intention to continue conducting attacks without regard to non-combatant casualties.[29] As a result, the use of force against Al Qaeda (and the Taliban) within Afghanistan, while not intended to avert a specific, imminent attack, met traditional legal requirements. Such uses of preventive force differ from uses of force intended to prevent a threat that has not matured to the point of acts of hostility. Al Qaeda's many attacks on the United States, accompanied by its leaders' declarations that "war" or "jihad" will continue to be waged against its enemies, justified treating the threat posed by that group as an ongoing, armed conflict, at least within Afghanistan

On September 18, 2001, the U.S. Congress did just that by conferring authority on the president to use force against "Al Qaeda" and "those responsible" for the attacks of September 11.[30]

The ensuing and continuing military engagement in Afghanistan is an armed conflict, in which anticipatory force is a lawful tool. To characterize the ensuing effort against Al Qaeda and other terrorist groups throughout the world as a "war" properly distinguishes it from conventional law enforcement activities. But that characterization cannot transform all Al Qaeda activities, wherever they occur, into aspects of the ongoing armed conflict in Afghanistan. Declaring a "war" on terror based on the conduct of Al Qaeda in Afghanistan does not establish, for example, that all suspected terrorists and their sponsors might lawfully be attacked in the same manner as combatants in an armed conflict elsewhere. Even if a suspected terrorist in a State other than Afghanistan is identified as a member of Al Qaeda, that fact alone would not justify using force against the suspect. Otherwise, an armed conflict could be claimed to exist in any State in which a combatant could be found, a position for which no authority exists, even with regard to combatants in conventional conflicts. The only possible justification for a preventive use of force within a State that has taken no part in an armed conflict would be that the State was unwilling or unable to fulfill its international obligations to deny support for, and to prevent attacks by, the suspected terrorist.[31] That argument has not been accepted as legally justifying the use of force.[32]

An exception to this general observation could exist if a terrorist group assumed control of some portion of a sovereign State and was using it as a base for illegal attacks. If the Taliban and/or Al Qaeda took control of part of Pakistan, for example, and launched attacks from that area into Afghanistan, their activities could reasonably be considered an extension of the armed conflict in Afghanistan, in which preventive uses of force are lawful. Israel regards the military struggle with Palestinian militants as an armed conflict, and on this basis regularly targets individuals in the West Bank and Gaza who Israel has determined have attacked, or are likely to attack, Israel or its nationals. Israel's Supreme Court has ruled that targeting such individuals can be lawful in principle, because a civilian loses non-combatant status under the laws of war by participating in an armed conflict.[33]

International law also recognizes that States engaged in an armed conflict have a limited right to pursue combatants into the territory of other, neutral States, and have the right to prevent interference in the conflict by neutral States.[34] A State may, for example, have authority to pursue and attack combatants who cross into the waters of neutral States.[35] In addition, neutral States are obliged to prevent persons within their territories from actively assisting combatants in any State in which an armed conflict is underway. If a State fails to abide by this obligation, a State engaged in the armed conflict could reasonably claim the right to enter the neutral State's territory for the purpose of preventing such activities.[36] This claim was used by Thailand in 1995 when it pursued guerrillas into Burma after repeated calls on Burma to prevent the guerrillas from crossing the border into Thailand. The International Court of Justice ruled, however, in a suit by Congo against Uganda, that the right of self-defense may not be invoked in response to attacks by irregular forces not controlled by a State.[37]

TRANSNATIONAL USES OF PREVENTIVE FORCE IN THE ABSENCE OF ARMED CONFLICT

While preventive force is generally lawful when used in national law enforcement and armed conflict, as described above, its use by one State within the territory of another in the absence of armed conflict and without Security Council approval is generally illegal under international law. States have nonetheless often used force without Security Council approval to prevent harm in various contexts, just as they have for other reasons that have been widely accepted, such as to expel colonial powers and in border disputes.[38] This section reviews the situations in which States have used preventive force since the adoption of the UN Charter. The frequency with which various types of preventive actions are undertaken, and the extent to which they are accepted in the international community, differ greatly, even though few if any of these uses of force can be defended as legal under international law.[39]

Prevention of Harm to Nationals

International law recognizes that States have the right and duty to protect their nationals, and States have often justified using force within the territory of other States on this basis.[40] Actions for the purpose of preventing harm to nationals were common before the UN Charter's adoption, and have continued in the post-Charter period. Even when nationals are genuinely in danger, however, this rationale for using force is often regarded in the international community as a pretext for achieving other, less legitimate aims, especially by major powers in their so-called spheres of influence. Some interventions are widely regarded as having been designed to influence the form of government of the targeted State.

A prominent and questionable invocation of the ground of protecting nationals took place in 1956 when Great Britain, France, and Israel intervened in Egypt and assumed control of the Suez Canal. Israel claimed it was responding to terrorist attacks encouraged by Egypt along its border in the Sinai. Great Britain and France claimed they had intervened for the purpose of protecting their nationals in the area, and to prevent the escalation of conflicts between Egyptian and Israeli forces. International criticism, led by the United States, caused the three States to withdraw. Governments and commentators generally believed that Great Britain and France acted in order to maintain control of the Canal, rather than to protect their nationals or to maintain peace.[41]

Belgium intervened in the Congo in July 1960, after granting it independence, when an army mutiny threatened 100,000 Belgian nationals in that country. The Security Council created a mission to assist the Congo and called on Belgium to withdraw its forces. Withdrawal finally took place in September 1960 after considerable criticism in the United Nations aimed mostly at the infliction by Belgian forces of substantial casualties. Belgium intervened in the Congo again in 1978 (then known as Zaire), along with France, to protect Congo's president and government. Belgium stated that its purpose was solely to protect its nationals, but France's stated goals included both the protection of nationals and the reestablishment of security.[42] Turkey intervened in Cyprus in 1964 and again in 1974 to protect the security and rights of ethnic Turks after Greek Cypriots violated the Treaty of Guarantee. Criticism focused on ending hostilities and on the claim that Turkey had assumed control over a greater area, and remained in control for longer, than required to protect the rights of ethnic Turks.[43]

The United States intervened in the Dominican Republic in 1965 during an insurrection by a radical group, citing the need to protect its nationals, but also noting the need to put down a "communist" uprising. The intervention effectively protected the U.S. nationals there, but also restored control to the prior government. The OAS adopted a resolution "regretting" the intervention, with only the United States dissenting.[44] In 1983 the United States intervened in Grenada after a coup by military officers supported by the Castro regime in Cuba. The United States based its intervention on the danger to several hundred of its nationals (including many medical students) but also cited both an invitation from the Governor General of Grenada to intervene, and support from the Organization of Eastern Caribbean States. The coup's leaders rejected a U.S. offer not to intervene if it were allowed to remove all its nationals.[45] The U.S. intervention, joined by small contingents from Jamaica and Barbados, effectively protected U.S. nationals but also gave the United States full control over the island; within two months it had removed all Cuban influence and installed a politically moderate government.[46]

The United States intervened in Panama in 1989, citing the threats made by President Manuel Noriega to kill U.S. troops and nationals (at least one U.S. soldier was killed), Noriega's drug dealing, his illegitimacy as a ruler (having refused to recognize the results of a UN-supervised election that should have removed him from office), and the invitation to intervene by the winner of that election, Guillermo Endara. U.S. forces established control, released an American hostage, and installed Endara as president. Noriega sought refuge in the Vatican's diplomatic mission, but eventually surrendered. He was removed to the United States for trial and convicted of drug dealing.[47] President Bush and other leaders noted that the removal of Noriega ensured that the U.S. commitment to surrender the Panama Canal would be implemented, and the Canal was turned over to the restored Panamanian government on schedule.[48] These U.S. actions received little international support, even though U.S. nationals were genuinely in danger in each instance and the interventions had considerable support in the States in which they occurred. Many governments and commentators believed the claimed purpose of protecting nationals was an excuse to replace governments the United States opposed with governments it favored.[49]

A credible claim of intervention for the purpose of protecting nationals took place in 1994, when the United States, France, and Belgium intervened in Rwanda to evacuate their citizens as violence began to spread, leading ultimately to the genocidal murder of some 800,000 Tutsis. The intervention provided security for the removal of several hundred foreigners, after which the three powers left the country without attempting to prevent the humanitarian disaster that was underway.[50]

The credibility of claims by States that they used force to prevent harm to their nationals is enhanced when the nationals are illegally held as hostages and appear in danger of harm. Nonetheless, transnational efforts to rescue hostages are sometimes condemned as illegal or viewed with suspicion. In 1964, rebels under Christopher Gbenye seized Stanleyville, in the Congo, and announced that 1,300 foreigners, including 600 Belgians, would not be permitted to leave. After two months of fruitless negotiations, the existing government under Moise Tshombe requested Belgium and the United States to help free the hostages. U.S. planes dropped 600 Belgian paratroopers into the area. They put an end to the rebellion and left the country. Only two of fifteen Security Council members argued the intervention was illegal, but a resolution was adopted calling for an end to interventions in the Congo, and several States claimed to view the intervention as an effort to preserve a pro-colonial government. In 1978, at the invitation of President Mobutu Sese Seko, and with U.S. help, Belgium and France intervened in the Congo (then Zaire) after a rebel group targeted foreign nationals. The Organization of African Unity (OAU) criticized the action as "gunboat diplomacy" aimed at propping up a corrupt regime, and announced its opposition to all foreign intervention in African conflicts.[51]

In 1969, El Salvador invaded Honduras after the latter removed many Salvadoran nationals from land they were farming and allegedly mistreated them. OAS pressure led El Salvador to withdraw its forces. The United States engaged in a major military effort in 1975, immediately after withdrawing from Vietnam, to rescue the crew of a U.S. merchant vessel, the SS *Mayaguez*, after Cambodian forces seized it. The ship's crew was released soon after fighting began, but the United States was not advised of this fact and continued its attack, suffering considerable losses but receiving no significant international criticism.[52] In 1977, Somalia invaded the Ogaden district of Ethiopia, allegedly to protect ethnic Somalis, but perhaps more likely to join the Western Somali Liberation Front in an effort to conquer the area. The parties eventually stopped fighting in 1988.[53]

The rescue by Israel in 1976 of 103 hostages from Entebbe, Uganda, is a particularly well-known hostage rescue. It illustrates the legal and legitimacy issues associated with entering a foreign State for that purpose. The hostages were seized in a joint operation by Germany's Baader-Meinhof Gang and the Popular Front for the Liberation of Palestine (PFLP) by hijacking a civilian aircraft, in violation of a widely adopted treaty. Jewish passengers were separated from the others, who were released. The hijackers landed the plane in Uganda and the Idi Amin government took control of the hostages rather than fulfilling its treaty obligation to release them. Amin threatened that the hostages would remain captive unless various demands were met.[54] Israel sent a commando force into the airport at which the hostages were being held, killed ten Ugandan guards, and flew all but one of the hostages to Israel. (The sole victim was a woman who had been taken to a hospital when she became sick; she was murdered after the hostages had been rescued.) The action was unanimously condemned by the OAU, including Kenya, which had permitted Israel to refuel its planes on the way home from the operation.[55] The rescue was praised by the United States and other States, however, and is now widely viewed as legitimate, if not lawful,[56] in light of the urgent need to protect civilians from a government leader known to be violent and irrational, and because of its limited nature and duration.

The United States attempted on April 24, 1980, to rescue fifty-two hostages seized by Iranian radicals from the U.S. embassy in Tehran.[57] The hostages were held by the Khomeini regime for several months, in violation of conventions against hostage-taking and the seizure of persons with diplomatic protection. The rescue effort failed and was criticized by many States, though it was supported by the United Kingdom, Egypt, and Israel. The USSR called the rescue a "pretext," despite the fact that the type and amount of force used could have had no other purpose.[58] The failed rescue led the United States to form new, coordinated military groups to enhance its capacity to implement similar rescue operations. In October 1985, the

United States intercepted an Egyptian military plane carrying Palestinian terrorists who had hijacked the Italian cruise ship, *Achille Lauro*, and murdered a physically disabled American passenger. The plane was forced to land at a NATO base in Italy. Although senior members of the terrorist group were released, several of the hijackers were prosecuted and served substantial sentences. The U.S. operation was intended to punish and thereby deter future hijacking operations. The United States also wished to demonstrate the unacceptability of agreements such as the one negotiated by Egypt to convince the hijackers to surrender to the Egyptian government in exchange for transporting them to the Palestine Liberation Organization (PLO) headquarters in Tunis, a breach of Egypt's obligation to prosecute or extradite such individuals.[59]

Seizure of hostages has become one of the principal tools of guerrillas in countries like Colombia. The Revolutionary Armed Forces of Colombia (FARC) has made a business of and gained political leverage by seizing individuals and holding them within Colombia or taking them to camps in Ecuador. Guerrilla forces in the Philippines have used this method to gain attention and ransoms. Pirates off the coasts of several States, including Somalia, Nigeria, and Indonesia, have seized hundreds of merchant vessels and have held the ships and their crews hostage in exchange for ransoms. A Security Council resolution authorizing pursuit of the Somali pirates into Somali waters has been used to protect food shipments to refugees in Somalia. Apparently, the fear that crew members will be killed and possible legal objections to acting within Somali waters or territory have caused States to limit their actions to defending vessels not yet seized, rather than attempting to recapture ships and crews or destroying pirate vessels and their encampments on the Somali shore.[60] In April 2009, the U.S. Navy rescued the captain of an American flagged vessel, the *Maersk Alabama*, killing two pirates and capturing one in the process.[61] While the legality of attacking pirates on the high seas is well established, attacks on pirates in Somali territory have by implication been disallowed by Security Council resolutions adopted to deal with the piracy issue.[62]

The Israeli/Palestinian conflict has resulted in many situations in which individuals are seized and held as hostages. The Hamas government in Gaza (or one of its allied groups), for example, seized an Israeli soldier in a cross-border raid in 2006 and demanded, in exchange for his release, that Israel release hundreds of prisoners, many of whom had been convicted of murdering Israeli noncombatants within Israeli territory.[63] Israel has itself seized individuals and held them to exchange for Israeli captives or their remains. Most notoriously, Israel seized Hezbollah's spiritual leader Sheikh Abdel Karim Obeid in 1989, describing the seizure as intended to force an exchange for Israeli soldiers captured during the 1981 war in Lebanon.[64]

During the summer of 2006, Hezbollah guerrillas from southern Lebanon attacked a small Israeli force within Israel, near a contested area, killing several soldiers and seizing two. Israel demanded release of its soldiers and reacted with an air and ground assault on Hezbollah installations and other targets, including an oil depot on the Mediterranean coast, bridges, and transportation infrastructure. Hezbollah responded by firing thousands of rockets at civilian centers in Israel. The conflict was brought to a negotiated halt through Security Council Resolution 1701 (adopted on August 11, 2006), introducing an international force at the Lebanon/Israel border to separate the hostile parties, but leaving the hostage issue unresolved. The Israeli action initially received some support in the Security Council and elsewhere, but this support largely dissipated as the action expanded in scope and duration.

Abductions (Transnational "Arrests")

Limited uses of force are sometimes undertaken by States in other States to capture individuals believed to have engaged in illegal conduct. The individuals seized in this manner are generally brought back to the State in which the alleged crimes occurred in order to be tried and punished. Abductions resemble domestic law enforcement activity, and often have the same purposes. But a State has no authority to enforce its law in another State without the latter's consent. Even if a State adopts a statute purporting to authorize foreign enforcement of its laws (as has often been done), these laws cannot alter the fact that unconsented uses of force undertaken within the territory of another State violate the laws of that State, and are widely recognized as violating international law.[65]

Despite the clear illegality of unconsented transnational law enforcement activities, States still occasionally abduct individuals they believe have violated their laws (in effect treating such actions as "arrests"). States that succeed in such abductions often refuse to return the individuals, even though they may recognize the illegality of their conduct and apologize for having violated the other State's sovereign territory. So pervasive has this practice been that international law has an established doctrine—*male captus, bene detentus* (bad capture, good detention)—to describe, if not to approve, the abductions.[66]

A high degree of tolerance appears to exist for abductions where the evidence is strong that the individual seized and prosecuted is guilty of serious criminal activity and the State from which the abduction occurred would have been unlikely to prosecute or extradite. Israel's abduction of Adolf Eichmann was found to be illegal and a breach of Argentina's sovereignty, but the Security Council refused Argentina's request to order Israel to return him.[67] Israel's apology was treated as a sufficient remedy, though the Council resolved that "if repeated" such violations of sovereignty might become a breach of international peace and security. By contrast, the U.S.-supported abduction of Dr. Alvarez-Machain from Mexico for allegedly participating in the torture of drug enforcement agents was upheld by the U.S. Supreme Court but had little if any international support. His acquittal after trial in the United States undermined the credibility of the operation.[68]

Efforts to capture individuals in foreign territory have sometimes been based on faulty intelligence, or go badly awry. Israel intercepted an Iraqi civilian airliner in Lebanese airspace in 1973 in an
effort to capture George Habash, head of the PFLP, forcing the plane
to land in Israel. Habash was not on the plane, and Israel's action
was condemned by the Security Council and the International Civil
Aviation Authority (ICAO), although no sanction was imposed. Israel intercepted a Libyan aircraft over international waters in 1986,
forcing it to land in Israel, in the belief that it was carrying Palestinian terrorists. No terrorists were on the plane and it was permitted
to fly on to Syria. A Security Council resolution condemning Israel's
action was vetoed by the United States on the grounds that an interception over international waters to capture terrorists, with no use
of force, was legally defensible.[69] Egypt sent seventy-five commandos
to Cyprus to prevent the escape of two Palestinians who had killed
a high-ranking Egyptian official. The Palestinians had been allowed
to leave Cyprus once before, but had not been able to land anywhere
else and had returned, so Egypt believed they would be allowed to
escape again. The Cypriot National Guard fired on the Egyptian
commandos, killed or wounded several, and destroyed their plane,
though Cyprus later tried the two Palestinians and sentenced them
to life imprisonment.[70]

Sometimes States abduct their own nationals, either for violating
laws or for otherwise displeasing the governing regimes. Among the
categories of persons seized by States for repatriation and punishment
are political enemies in hiding; individuals granted political asylum;
spies believed to be double agents; and tyrants who absconded with
illegitimately acquired riches. All these actions are considered illegal and have little international support. Some abductions are so
universally disfavored that they have been made into international
crimes, prohibited by specific international conventions, including
the hijacking of planes or ships,[71] the seizure of diplomats,[72] and the

deliberate taking of an individual as a hostage to be held for ransom or for a political purpose or exchange.[73]

Targeted Killings

The deliberate killing of specific individuals takes place in national law enforcement and armed conflict, subject to established rules such as the requirement that the use of deadly force be both reasonable and necessary. Such actions are frequently preventive in purpose, in that they seek to stop individuals from continuing their attacks and also to deter others from such conduct. A recent example of a targeted killing in an armed conflict is the bombing by the United States of a house in which the leader of Al Qaeda in Iraq, Abu Musab al-Zarqawi, was consulting with his spiritual adviser.[74]

Targeted killings that cannot be justified as national law enforcement or as part of an armed conflict are widely regarded as unlawful unless conducted with the territorial State's consent. The United States had Yemen's consent to use a rocket from an unmanned aircraft to kill one of the perpetrators of the attack on the USS *Cole*. It has also used such aircraft and conventional bombings to kill particular Al Qaeda and Taliban members in Pakistan near the Afghan border, at times apparently with the consent of both governments.

Targeted killings are defended as lawful when undertaken to prevent operations from a State that has refused or is unable to stop the targeted individual's illegal activities. U.S. officials attempted to target Osama bin Laden and other Al Qaeda leaders on several occasions before September 11, 2001, but were unable to implement this plan.[75] In the presidential campaign of 2008, the Democratic Party candidate, Senator Barack Obama, announced his intention as president to find and kill bin Laden and other leaders who attacked America, without Pakistan's permission if necessary. The Republican candidate, Senator John McCain, agreed that such actions were necessary, arguing only that they should not be announced to avoid embarrassing an ally. Attacks by the United States on militants in Pakistan have been frequent, despite objections by the Pakistani government and significant collateral deaths and injuries.

Israel has used targeted killing in Lebanon against leaders of Hezbollah; on February 16, 1992, for example, an Israeli rocket destroyed a car in southern Lebanon, killing Sheikh Abbas Musawi and his family.[76] Targeted killing in such situations, in the absence of an ongoing armed conflict, may be justified as actions in self-defense if the individual targeted has previously attacked the targeting State and is expected to do so again, and if no other means exists of preventing him from doing so.[77] But such actions are clear cases of prevention rather than preemption, when no attack is imminent.

The non-consensual violation of a sovereign State's territory is not the only ground on which targeted killings are criticized. Some critics characterize targeted killings as "non-judicial executions," since they are typically undertaken without formal trials or specific determinations of guilt. They are therefore sometimes condemned as violations of due process, even when conducted within a national territory, or with the consent of the territorial state. Targeted killings may also be opposed due to the unintended deaths of innocent individuals, because of mistaken identity, erroneous judgment, and collateral damage.

These criticisms of targeted killings are weighty but largely applicable to the use of deadly force in any context. States "target" criminal suspects in the course of law enforcement activities, for example, as well as enemy combatants during armed conflict, without having conducted formal trials in advance. In both contexts, mistakes are made; innocent people are targeted in error; collateral damage results. But the officials or military personnel involved are generally immune from prosecution if they acted in good faith.

A high degree of accountability is imposed by law and treaty, however, in both national law enforcement and armed conflict compared to the limited regulation of targeted killing. Actions in law enforcement and armed conflict are usually conducted openly, moreover, and acknowledged by the governments involved; targeted killings are conducted secretly and often without acknowledgment. In response to this comparative lack of legal accountability, some States that rely on targeted killings have established standards and procedures to enhance their fairness, justifiability, accuracy, and discriminate implementation.

First, limits have been placed on the grounds upon which a person may be targeted. For example, in the United States, targeted killings are unlawful when they constitute "assassination,"[78] which is considered equivalent to murder.[79] The United States distinguishes assassinations from the killing (in self-defense) of individuals who have attacked Americans and are likely to do so again.[80] Other States have targeted political enemies, and some continue to do so.[81] But no State has attempted to defend political killings as lawful or legitimate.

A second type of restraint on targeted killing attempts to minimize errors and collateral damage by establishing processes to evaluate legal, political, and ethical consequences. Israel's Supreme Court has imposed evidentiary and procedural standards on Israeli officials that must be met.[82] The United States has similar prerequisites.[83] Israel defends its attacks in Gaza and the West Bank as effective, with few collateral injuries.[84] Targeted killings are in fact generally limited operations, causing fewer collateral consequences and civilian injuries than conventional attacks.

Another form of restraint on targeted killings (and on any other use of preventive force) is financial accountability. Israel publicly apologized and paid compensation for the successful targeted killing of a terrorist in Gaza which used a bomb so large that it destroyed an entire building, killing numerous innocent civilians. NATO forces operating in Afghanistan and U.S. forces in Iraq also pay compensation to families adversely affected by attacks.

Restraints on targeted killing are less effective if such attacks are conducted in secret because they receive less scrutiny within governments than avowed actions. They are usually kept secret, not only from the outside world, but also from government officials whose normal duties would otherwise extend to reviewing their propriety. Israel adopted new policies regarding targeted killing after its secret service attempted to kill Hamas leader Khaled Mashaal in Jordan.[85] The action was politically ill-considered and poorly implemented, resulting in the arrest of two Israeli agents (for whom a costly exchange was made) and the disruption of relations with Jordan.

Transnational, targeted killings are likely to continue to be used by States seeking to prevent attacks where no alternative exists and the collateral consequences are limited. The development of principles and procedures that regulate targeted killing should provide some protection against their inappropriate use. But resort to this type of preventive force will continue to be widely condemned as illegal and prone to unacceptable risks of error and collateral damage.

Attacks on Non-state Actors and Infrastructure

Non-state actors, including terrorist groups, significantly enhance their potential to cause harm when States provide them with camps and other facilities in which to train members, secure resources, and base their operations. Al Qaeda was able to operate in Afghanistan with impunity for several years, even as it launched major attacks, including several against U.S. facilities and nationals. During that time it trained thousands of recruits in terrorist methods and acquired significant credibility among like-minded individuals and organizations worldwide. In some instances, non-state groups operate, not only with the territorial State's acquiescence and support, but also under its influence or control. Other groups operate independently, however, because the States in which they are located lack control over them (for example, Hezbollah in Lebanon or the Taliban in parts of Pakistan) or the territory in which they are located is not governed by a sovereign State (Hamas in Gaza).

Preventive attacks on non-state actors and their facilities in foreign States have been frequent. After many attacks by terrorists from Egypt during the 1950s, Israel launched an attack in the Sinai Peninsula in 1956 aimed at preventing future attacks. Palestinian attacks on Israel from Lebanon in 1974, which Lebanon could not prevent, led Israel to attack Palestinian and Lebanese targets. This action was widely criticized, and Security Council resolutions condemned both Israel and the Palestinian attacks.[86]

The United States attacked terrorist support facilities in Libya (1986) in response to State-supported terrorist attacks against U.S. nationals in the Rome and Vienna airports, and later at a Berlin discotheque. The United States justified its action as self-defense, noting that it had evidence that Libya had used the Abu Nidal terrorist group to conduct attacks on U.S. nationals, and was planning additional attacks on U.S. and allied targets. Targeting facilities in which terrorists were given training by the Libyan government was intended to reduce Libya's capacity and willingness to engage in such actions in the future.[87] The U.S. attack on Libya was nonetheless condemned as illegal by the UN General Assembly in a vote of 79–28, with 33 abstentions.[88] A Security Council resolution condemning the attack was vetoed by the United States, the United Kingdom, and France, although it received nine votes (the required majority).[89]

The United States attacked an Iraqi intelligence headquarters in 1993 in response to a State-supported effort to use terrorists to kill former U.S. President George H.W. Bush in Kuwait.[90] The United States viewed the building as a proper target because the attempted assassination had been planned by Iraqi intelligence. The United States attacked Al Qaeda training camps in Afghanistan in 1998 in response to attacks on U.S. nationals and facilities.[91] Israel attacked terrorist training camps in Lebanon (1982) and Syria (2003) and the PLO headquarters in Tunis (1985) in response to terrorist attacks and in order to deter future attacks.[92] Repeated Security Council resolutions called for the withdrawal of Israeli forces from Lebanon. But only after the assassination of Lebanese President Bashir Gemayel did the Security Council expressly condemn Israeli incursions in Beirut.[93] The Security Council voted to condemn Israel's attack on the PLO in Tunis as an act of aggression, with the United States abstaining on the ground that, while such attacks may be legally justified, this attack was damaging to relations with the Tunisian government.[94] The United States argued that Israel had exercised its right to self-defense in the 2003 bombing in Syria but called for restraint.[95] Israel reportedly conducted three military strikes in Sudanese territory in January and February 2009 against trucks (and a ship in the Red Sea) carrying weapons supplied by Iran for delivery to Hamas in Gaza. Sudanese officials said that thirty-nine people were killed and seventeen trucks destroyed in a single raid. Israeli officials refused to confirm responsibility, but Prime Minister Ehud Olmert stated on March 26: "Israel hits every place it can in order to stop terror, near and far."[96]

Uganda invaded and occupied more than one-third of the territory of the Democratic Republic of Congo (DRC) between 1998 and 2003, claiming it acted in self-defense against attacks by rebels who controlled that area of the DRC. Uganda relied on the ICJ's decision in *Corfu Channel* that held that States have "a duty of vigilance to ensure that such activities [as mining international waterways] are not tolerated."[97] In a suit by the DRC against Uganda, the ICJ held that the right to self-defense may not be asserted against attacks by a non-state group unless the group's conduct is attributable to the State from which the attacks were launched. For a State to be responsible for the acts of a non-state group within its territory, the Court held, the State's support for the group must itself amount to an "act of aggression," meaning that the group is "sent by or on behalf of a State" that exercises "effective control" to commit an illegal act.[98] The Court held that the DRC could not be held responsible for the rebel attacks, because it was unable to control the group that had attacked Uganda.[99] The Court failed to consider whether Uganda might be entitled to resort to proportional measures other than self-defense, apparently because it concluded that Uganda's conduct would in any event have exceeded what was necessary under the circumstances.[100]

In 1995, Turkish forces invaded northwestern Iraq to pursue Kurdish secessionists responsible for cross-border attacks into Turkey. Iraq objected, noting that it could do nothing about the rebels because of what it called illegal intervention by the United States and its allies in the Kurdish areas of Iraq. Turkey responded that Iraq was responsible nonetheless, and that it had no option but to engage in self-defense, having complained often and in vain. In 1996, Turkey again used force in Iraq, and Iraq filed a complaint in the Security Council and with the Secretary-General of the United Nations. Neither the Council nor the General Assembly held a meeting on the issue. That same year, Iran pursued Kurdish rebels into Iraq and bombed their bases there, with no international response.[101] During 2007 and 2008, Turkish forces again attacked Kurdish rebels within Iraq in response to cross-border raids and terrorist bombings in Turkey. The new Iraqi government complained, but sought no formal international condemnation or other relief. All these raids were conducted in a discriminate manner consistent with the limited objective of preventing future attacks.[102]

In March 2008, Colombia attacked members of the Revolutionary Armed Forces of Colombia (FARC) at a base located in Ecuador, killing FARC's leader, Raul Reyes, and twenty other rebels. Colombia claimed it had acted in self-defense, and that Ecuador (along with Venezuela) had been assisting FARC in its rebellion against the Colombian government. Colombia also claimed its forces had seized computers and CDs that established that FARC received assistance from both the Ecuadorean and Venezuelan governments. Ecuador and Venezuela protested this action and moved troops to their borders with Colombia, threatening military action. Ecuador demanded that the Organization of American States (OAS) condemn Colombia's action

Colombia apologized for violating Ecuador's territorial sovereignty and suggested that it did not plan to engage in such actions in the future. The OAS adopted a resolution characterizing the intrusion as a violation of international law and invoking the OAS Charter provision prohibiting in absolute terms any violation by a member State of the sovereign territory of another. But the OAS did not issue a condemnation of Colombia's conduct.[103]

Recent UN Security Council resolutions make clear that States are obligated to prevent terrorists from having access to support facilities within their territories. Under current international legal standards, however, these resolutions provide no legal support for using force to attack terrorist infrastructure in States that fail to prevent the launch of attacks from within their borders. Current standards require that the Security Council must separately and expressly authorize every use of force not amounting to self-defense, even to curb clear violations of existing resolutions. The ICJ's decision in *DRC v. Uganda* further restricts a State's right of self-defense (if not the use of force altogether) against non-state actors in the sovereign territory of another State to situations where the territorial State is responsible for the attack.[104] Nonetheless, States seem unlikely to refrain entirely from attacks in foreign States against terrorist training facilities. Such attacks have received at least some acceptance within the international community when they are limited in nature and duration and when they are intended to prevent future attacks rather than to acquire territory, control resources, or achieve any other improper purpose.

Actions to Prevent Subversion

Some of the most significant uses of force in the post-Charter period have been for the purpose of preventing the subversion of an existing regime. While it is illegal to attempt to subvert a recognized government by supporting rebels with military and logistical assistance, international law does not necessarily treat such support as an attack justifying resort to force in self-defense. Many States have nonetheless used force to prevent subversion by attacking the rebels involved or the States that support them, and have often sought assistance from other States in doing so.

An early and important instance of this type of action was the U.S.-led effort to prevent the Greek Communist Party (KKE) from winning a civil war against the Greek government with the assistance of its Communist allies: Albania, Bulgaria, and Yugoslavia. President Harry S. Truman considered State support for the KKE a form of aggression for which the Soviet Union was ultimately responsible. He was determined to prevent the overthrow of the Greek government and provided substantial military support that enabled the Greek government to defeat the KKE by 1949.[105] An effort by Nicaragua in 1948 (under President Anastasio Somoza Garcia) to overthrow the Costa Rican government by giving military support to rebels within that country was stopped through OAS action and U.S. assistance. The United States provided military assistance to the Republic of China (Taiwan) in 1958 when the People's Republic of China attacked the Quemoy and Matsu Islands; the PRC backed off, retaining its claim, however, to those islands and to Taiwan itself.

Egypt intervened militarily during the Yemeni Civil War, 1962–1970, allegedly to prevent attacks by Saudi Arabia and Jordan, but in reality to overthrow the Imam Al-Badr.[106] After several years, a regime emerged that negotiated a coalition among contesting forces and the war ended. Communist rebels fought a civil war from 1965 to 1976 to replace the Sultan of Oman, with military support from South Yemen and other communist regimes. The Sultan's son removed his father, implemented reforms, and defeated the rebels with the help of the United Kingdom, Iran, Pakistan, and Jordan.[107] In 1963, an arms cache supplied by the Cuban government to assist the Venezuelan Communist Party's attempt to overthrow the government was discovered in Venezuela. The OAS called on all its members to break relations with Cuba over this intervention, which all did in 1964 except for Mexico. Cuba tried again in 1966 to overthrow the Venezuelan government by sending rebels and trained officers into the country. The operation ended after the OAS objected; no sanctions were imposed.

Many States intervened during the civil war in Chad between 1969 and 1993, most notably Libya, with supplies from the USSR. France came to Chad's defense at the request of President Hissene Habre, leading Libya ultimately to resolve its border dispute with Chad at the ICJ. Syria assisted Palestinians in Jordan in 1970 when they attempted to overthrow its government, sending arms and tanks Syria claimed were assets of the Palestinian Liberation Army.[108] Jordan defeated the rebellion and drove the Palestinian refugees who had participated out of the country into Lebanon. Israel threatened to intervene on Jordan's behalf if Syria persisted in its effort. Civil wars in Africa during the 1970s also attracted interventions by States acting on the side of the rebels or the established regimes, including uprisings in Mozambique (1975–92), Angola (1975–76), Zaire (1977), and Tunisia (1980). The Security Council condemned South Africa for intervening in Angola, but otherwise these civil wars were resolved through the use of force and diplomacy.

The United States intervened in El Salvador at its government's request to assist it in defeating rebels supported by Nicaragua. The United States supplied funds and materials to El Salvador and also to rebels within Nicaragua who were themselves attempting to overthrow its left-wing elected regime.[109] The United States also mined Nicaragua's harbors to block supplies from Cuba and elsewhere. Nicaragua sued the United States in the ICJ, claiming it had acted illegally by assisting El Salvador through its support of the rebels within Nicaragua, including the mining of Nicaragua's harbors. The ICJ denied El Salvador's application to intervene in the action, and held that, even if Nicaragua had assisted rebels seeking to overthrow El Salvador's government by supplying arms, equipment, and other aid, the level of its assistance was insufficient to trigger El Salvador's right of self-defense. The significance of this ruling was that, while the right of self-defense would have entitled El Salvador to seek U.S. assistance by collectively exercising that right, El Salvador was instead restricted to engaging in "proportionate measures" to offset Nicaragua's efforts limited to its own sovereign territory. Furthermore, the ICJ held, any exercise of collective self-defense must be declared and reported to the Security Council in advance, which El Salvador failed to do with sufficient formality. Several judges dissented from some or all of these rulings. The ICJ unanimously concluded, however that, even assuming the United States was entitled to assist El Salvador in the collective exercise of its right of self-defense, some of the measures it adopted, in particular the mining of Nicaragua's harbors, were improper and disproportionate uses of force under international law.[110] U.S. support enabled El Salvador's government to prevail against the Nicaraguan-supported rebels. Daniel Ortega was voted out of office in Nicaragua in an election to which the contesting parties agreed as a means for ending the dispute. The newly elected government of Nicaragua issued an apology for the extensive assistance the former regime had provided to Salvadoran rebels, after a major cache of Nicaraguan weapons was discovered within El Salvador in November 1989.[111]

Attacks against WMD Development and Facilities

The danger that irresponsible regimes and terrorist groups may acquire weapons of mass destruction is frequently advanced as justifying preventive force. Several States have acquired WMD in the years since the United States developed nuclear weapons. But force has seldom been used to attempt to prevent such developments.

During the 1950s, the U.S. government considered using force to prevent first the USSR and later China from acquiring nuclear weapons. In both cases, the United States decided against using preventive force. While both the USSR and China were regarded as potential strategic threats, no specific evidence indicated that either State intended to use nuclear weapons (or other WMD) against the United States or any other State. In both instances, the case for using force was based on preventing those States from acquiring *the capacity* to destroy or seriously damage the United States or to challenge U.S. hegemony. These dangers were considered insufficient to justify launching preventive attacks in light of the expected costs and consequences.[112] The United States also refrained from a preventive attack during the Cuban missile crisis to avoid escalating a confrontation with the USSR that was instead resolved through a blockade and diplomacy.[113]

As North Korea moved toward developing a nuclear device in violation of its obligations under the Nuclear Non-Proliferation Treaty (NPT), the United States, with considerable international support, threatened sanctions and even military force if the program continued.[114] Sanctions were imposed but no military action was taken although North Korea proceeded to develop and test a nuclear device.[115] National security planners generally agree that the United States could have destroyed North Korea's nuclear facilities.[116] They also agree that during such a conflict the North could have inflicted grave damage on South Korea with artillery bombardments, resulting in one million or more casualties.[117] These costs may explain why the United States has continued to pursue a course based on the combined diplomatic and economic efforts of several interested States, including China, with the objective of convincing North Korea to give up its nuclear facilities and, ultimately, the nuclear weapons it has made.[118] Even the more limited objective of preventing North Korea from illegally transferring nuclear technology and WMD capacities to other States presents significant danger, since the North Korean government has issued a warning that it will treat stopping its vessels in international waters as an attack.[119]

The clearest instance in which force was used to prevent the acquisition of nuclear weapons was in 1981 when Israel attacked the Osirik Reactor to prevent Iraq from developing the capacity to produce plutonium. (Iran had attacked the facility in September 1980 during its war with Iraq, but ineffectually.)[120] Iraq claimed the purpose of the plant was to produce electrical power, and that in any event Israel had no right to prevent Iraq from developing arms of any sort in the absence of an actual or imminent attack. Israel noted that Iraq had repeatedly attacked Israel in the past; that Iraq had insisted on remaining in a state of war with Israel; and that Iraq continued to call for the destruction of Israel. Israel's action was taken before the threat from Iraq's nuclear program had become imminent. But Israel justified the action as necessary to avoid attacking the plant after it had been put into operation, when radiation would have been dispersed. The Security Council condemned Israel's attack as a "clear violation" of the Charter (Resolution 487, June 19, 1981). In recent years, however, some government officials and scholars have defended the attack as justified by the circumstances, and as having ensured that Saddam Hussein's subsequent aggressions were not accompanied by the threat or use of nuclear weapons.[121]

Israel bombed a site in Syria on September 6, 2007, claiming the facility was intended for nuclear weapons-related work undertaken with North Korean assistance. Syria protested the attack, denying that the site was related to nuclear activities. Syria sought General Assembly condemnation of Israel's conduct, but has refused to permit access to the site by international inspectors.[122]

The United States attacked a plant in Sudan in 1998 that it believed was under the control of allies of Al Qaeda and was engaged in producing chemicals for use in weapons. Sudan and the plant owner objected, claiming that the plant did not manufacture the chemicals alleged, and was a private facility producing pharmaceuticals.[123]

The most substantial military action intended to prevent the development of WMD was the intervention by the United States and several allied States into Iraq in 2003. The intervention followed sixteen Security Council resolutions commencing after Iraq's defeat by a UN-approved force in 1991 and condemning (among other things) Iraq's failure to comply with the demands of United Nations weapons inspectors. None of the resolutions explicitly authorized the use of force in Iraq. The invading States claimed, however, that Security Council resolutions related to Iraq's suspected possession of WMD implicitly authorized the intervention.[124] An additional reason was to prevent Iraq from providing weapons to terrorist groups that could use them against the United States and its allies.[125] Also cited was Saddam Hussein's illegal development of chemical weapons and his use of them against Iran and his own people, as well as his continuing violations of human rights through mass murder and torture of his political enemies. No illegal WMD were discovered in Iraq.

Libya conducted a program intended to develop nuclear weapons for several years, with the assistance of Pakistan's nuclear weapons program director A.Q. Kahn, North Korea, and others.[126] The United States and other States threatened to use force to prevent Libya from acquiring nuclear weapons. Proof of the program's existence was established by the seizure of the vessel BBC *China* carrying equipment intended for its advancement.[127] After negotiations conducted by several States with Libya, President Muammar Qaddafi agreed to give up Libya's nuclear weapons program as part of an arrangement that included Libya's acceptance of responsibility for the Pan Am 103 bombing and the lifting of sanctions against the regime.[128]

The current WMD threat most often advanced as potentially requiring the use of preventive force is Iran's program to enrich uranium.[129] Iran has claimed that its program is lawful and is intended to supply Iran with nuclear power for civilian purposes, a right it enjoys under the Non-Proliferation Treaty, which Iran has ratified. The Security Council found that Iran misled investigators and illegally acquired equipment and capacities. But the Council imposed sanctions widely regarded as weak. Iran insists that it will continue to develop the capacity to enrich uranium, despite statements by various governments and their leaders, including U.S. presidents and Israeli prime ministers, that they will not allow Iran to acquire nuclear weapons.[130] Iran has simultaneously developed increasingly long-range missiles, which within a few years are expected to be able to carry nuclear weapons or other WMD as far as Europe. Iran has also promised to respond to any attack with every means at its disposal, including mining the Strait of Hormuz to prevent the transfer of oil from the Persian Gulf. National security experts agree that eliminating Iran's capacity to enrich will be difficult, costly, unpopular in Iran, and likely to lead Iran to build the same capacity in places that will be more difficult to destroy. U.S. Secretary of Defense Robert Gates has warned against an Israeli strike on Iran's nuclear facilities for essentially these reasons.[131] Some experts say that any hope of a transition in Iran to more democratic and responsible institutions would be seriously damaged by a preventive attack on its nuclear facilities. Many agree, however, that without some change in its current course, Iran is likely to gain the capacity to produce, and that it may go on to acquire, nuclear weapons. This outcome is viewed by some as more dangerous than the consequences of attempting to prevent Iran's acquisition of nuclear weapons.[132]

North Korea and Iran illustrate the difficulties in evaluating the need for preventive force to deal with acquisition of WMD by irresponsible regimes. Both cases pose grave potential threats to international peace and security. In both cases, however, resort to preventive force has substantial limitations, may prove extremely costly, and may be unnecessary. In both situations, the evidence on capacities and intentions is incomplete and contradictory, making it difficult to predict whether preventive action might ever be appropriate.

Another situation that could lead States to consider resorting to preventive force may arise if a government of a State possessing WMD loses its capacity to control them. If the government of Pakistan, for example, were replaced with a radical Islamic regime considered likely to use or transfer nuclear weapons to terrorist groups, threatened States might consider preventive measures, especially if the Security Council failed to act effectively

Humanitarian Intervention

Interventions with significant humanitarian benefits have taken place since the Charter's adoption. But humanitarian considerations have only recently taken on significant weight in the international community. India invaded East Pakistan in December 1971, for example, to end what it described as genocide and the forced displacement of eight million Bengalis (many of whom fled to India as refugees). India complained to the UN Security Council and Secretary General that gross violations of human rights were taking place in the area beginning in April 1971, but nothing was done to end the suffering although the Secretary General acknowledged the crisis. Pakistan rejected India's argument that the flow of refugees constituted aggression and insisted that the crisis was "internal." India stressed the humanitarian issue, arguing that territorial integrity was not the only value in the Charter, citing both the Genocide Convention and the principle of self-determination. The Security Council voted 12–2 to demand an immediate cessation of hostilities and withdrawal by each State of armed personnel from the territory of the other, a provision clearly aimed at India. The resolution was vetoed by the Soviet Union. The General Assembly voted 104–11, with 10 abstentions, for withdrawal of all armed forces. India persisted, defeated Pakistani forces, and assisted the area in seceding and establishing the country now known as Bangladesh. Recognition of Bangladesh was delayed until 1974, but otherwise no sanctions or other measures were taken against India for its action.[133]

Tanzania intervened militarily in Uganda in 1979 in response to border incursions by the Idi Amin regime in 1978 and to Uganda's formal annexation of Tanzanian territory across the Kagera River boundary on November 1, 1978. Tanzania claimed it was acting in self-defense, but its response was months after the incursions. It also cited the need to bring an end to President Amin's oppressive activities, which were estimated to have resulted in the murder of

300,000 people and the expulsion of all Asians. Uganda complained to the United Nations that Tanzania's action was a great danger to regional and international security, an act of aggression, and a violation of the sovereignty and territorial integrity of Uganda. Neither the Security Council nor the General Assembly convened a meeting or responded to Uganda's complaints. Only Libya joined Uganda in urging the United Nations to act (and in a futile effort to defend the Ugandan capital of Kampala). Although Tanzania had interests in removing Amin from power beyond the humanitarian objective of saving Uganda's people, it demonstrated that it had no territorial ambitions when it withdrew all its troops by May 1981, after a new Ugandan government restored order.[134]

Vietnam invaded Cambodia (Kampuchea) on December 25, 1978, defeated the Pol Pot regime, and installed a group of exiles as Cambodia's new government, replacing a regime that had become an instrument of China. Vietnam claimed that the Pol Pot regime had started a border war against Vietnam and that the invasion was an achievement of the Kampuchean people.[135] Cambodia, China, and most other States condemned the intervention as an aggression mounted in cooperation with the Soviet Union. China in fact launched what it termed a "punitive" mission against Vietnam, based on the latter's action in Kampuchea and border disputes; China withdrew its forces amid widespread calls for China's withdrawal after a month of intensive fighting in which the Chinese sustained significant casualties. Vietnam, and especially East Germany, noted that the Pol Pot regime pursued inhumane policies, turned the nation into a concentration camp, and committed massive violations of human rights. But, despite the strong evidence establishing the Cambodian government's gruesome record (including proof of the murder of one million people), most States, including those in the West, opposed the intervention. The French representative stated, for example, that the "notion that because a regime is detestable foreign intervention is justified and forcible overthrow is legitimate is extremely dangerous. That could ultimately jeopardize the very maintenance of international law and order and make the continued existence of various regimes dependent on the judgment of their neighbours."[136] A Security Council resolution calling on Vietnam to withdraw secured thirteen votes in favor, but was vetoed by the Soviet Union. The General Assembly insisted on the right of the Khmer Rouge to govern Cambodia until 1988. Vietnam kept its troops in Cambodia until a UN-supervised election in 1993, adding evidence to the strongly felt conclusion by most States that, although Vietnam had replaced a brutal regime, it had done so for its own strategic reasons and not in order to prevent further repression.[137]

France assisted in removing Emperor Jean-Bedel Bokassa from power in the Central African Empire in September 1979. Judges from several African States concluded a month prior to the removal that Bokassa had ordered and participated in the massacre of 100 school children, and he reportedly engaged in many other atrocities within his country. France initially denied participating in the overthrow of Bokassa, engineered while he was visiting Libya. News reports revealed, however, that France offered the planners of the coup assistance if they deposed Bokassa. The French Foreign Ministry eventually confirmed the stories. Very few States complained of France's action, and no meeting of the Security Council or General Assembly addressed it.[138]

In 1991, immediately after Iraq was forced out of Kuwait by a UN-approved intervention, a crisis developed within Iraq when its Kurdish population revolted against Saddam Hussein's government. Repressive measures were immediately imposed, causing about one million Kurds to move toward the Turkish border in panic.[139] The Security Council condemned Iraq's repression of its civilian population as a threat to international peace and security, and called on Iraq to cooperate with humanitarian relief efforts. China made it clear it would veto any resolution authorizing intervention without Iraq's consent.[140] In April, the United States, Britain, and France, acting without either Iraqi or Security Council approval, declared the area north of the thirty-sixth parallel off limits to Iraqi forces. They began providing food and dispatched 10,000 troops to protect 700,000 Kurds.[141] The United Kingdom asserted that States have the right to intervene in situations where extreme humanitarian distress demands immediate relief, and when no practical alternative to intervention is available, but only to the extent necessary. U.S. Secretary of State Madeleine Albright announced that "while Washington would prefer to have the Council behind it, it is prepared to take punitive action alone."[142] The immediate need for troops to protect the relief operation was resolved in late May, when Iraq agreed to the deployment of 500 lightly armed UN guards for that purpose.

On August 24, 1990, the Economic Community of West African States (ECOWAS) decided to respond to a crisis in Liberia (one of its Member States) by forming a Cease-Fire Monitoring Group (ECO-MOG) to impose a truce among three groups fighting to control that government. The fighting displaced hundreds of thousands of civilians (including nationals of ECOWAS members), causing them and the conflict to spill into neighboring countries. Liberian President Samuel Doe had asked the organization in June 1990 to intervene to assist him in re-establishing control, but it instead deployed 15,000 mainly Nigerian troops, tanks, and aircraft to impose a ceasefire. A ceasefire was arranged in November 1990, after Doe was captured and killed by one of the groups seeking control. Regional organizations are encouraged in Article 53 of the UN Charter to assist in ensuring regional stability, but their enforcement actions are not to be taken "without the authorization of the Security Council." The Security Council nonetheless issued a Presidential Statement in January 1991 commending the efforts of the ECOWAS Heads of State, appearing to ratify the regional organization's unauthorized use of force retroactively. Renewed fighting in 1992 led ECOWAS to impose an embargo on supplies to the combatants, with the Security Council's support. The Council created a mission in 1993 to assist

ECOMOG's peacekeeping and peace-building activities, and a peace agreement was reached in 1996 that led to an election.[143]

A military coup in Sierra Leone (also a member of ECOWAS) in May 1997 unraveled a settlement that had ended tremendous human suffering and disruption caused by several years of civil war. The OAU called on ECOWAS to help the people of Sierra Leone "to restore the constitutional order."[144] The UN Security Council welcomed "mediation" efforts by ECOWAS, but did not authorize further intervention.[145] ECOWAS nonetheless went ahead with a military occupation of the capital, Freetown, and the imposition of sanctions.[146] The Security Council "took note" of the decision to impose sanctions and authorized their strict implementation, commending the "important role" that ECOWAS continued to play in bringing about a peaceful resolution. ECOMOG troops then forcibly ousted the military junta, seized control of the capital, and invited the exiled, elected president to resume his office. The Council unanimously approved this result and authorized a small number of UN military liaison personnel to "coordinate closely" with ECOMOG. After years of further conflict and difficulties, the Council approved a sizable force to assume responsibility for security, and stability was achieved in 2000.

In 1998, the Prime Minister of Lesotho urgently requested Member States of the South African Development Community (SADC) to intervene militarily in order to prevent a military coup, as he had lost control over Lesotho's armed forces. South African troops, together with members of Botswana's Defense Forces, entered Lesotho as an SADC force, pursuant to the obligation to prevent militaries from unconstitutionally overthrowing lawful regimes. Within a month, the parties in Lesotho resolved their differences and agreed to an election, after which the SADC forces withdrew. An election was held in 2002.[147]

NATO is responsible for perhaps the most significant unauthorized post-Charter humanitarian intervention when it bombed

Serbia to stop a campaign of violence and ethnic cleansing against Albanian Kosovars. Serbian President Slobodan Milosevic's effort to reverse the autonomy granted Kosovo in 1989 led to violent opposition from the Kosovo Liberation Army, which in turn led to the bombings and killings of Kosovars, including many civilians. The Security Council condemned the violence on both sides, reimposed an arms embargo, and called for an end to Serbian attacks on noncombatants. China and Russia made clear, however, that they would not permit a resolution authorizing the use of force against Serbia. A group of five NATO members (France, Germany, Italy, the United Kingdom, and the United States) proposed a plan to give Kosovo greater autonomy while maintaining Serbian sovereignty, but Serbia rejected the plan. By then, 600,000 Kosovars had fled to neighboring States and 800,000 more were being driven out of the country. NATO began its attacks, leading to a heated debate in the Security Council in which Russia, China, India, and some other States expressed their opposition to the action and to the idea of a right to intervene for humanitarian reasons without Council approval. Defenders of NATO avoided arguing self-defense or aggression based on the forced infliction of refugees on neighboring States. They focused instead on the legality or moral necessity of preventing a human catastrophe deliberately inflicted by a State on part of its own population. Some States supported the action on moral grounds, conceding that NATO had violated the Charter, but regretting that the Council had failed to perform its role of preventing further suffering. A resolution sponsored by Russia calling for the "immediate cessation" of NATO's "aggression" was voted down, 12–3.[148]

In March 2008, 750 Tanzanian troops, along with about 1,000 troops from Senegal, Sudan, and Comoros, intervened to depose Comoros President Mohamed Bacar, who refused to leave office after his term ended. Bacar, a former military leader, took control of the island of Anjouan, and the African Union approved a resolution to remove him by force if necessary. Just before the action commenced, President Mbeki of South Africa changed his position and opposed the intervention, urging further negotiations. The action went ahead, however, and Bacar was removed from power. He was replaced by the democratically elected Union Government led by President Ahmed Sambi.[149]

The post-Charter record establishes, therefore, that a considerable number of unauthorized interventions have prevented human suffering. Other instances of massive violations of human rights in that same period, however, resulted in no interventions by other States. The genocide of Tutsis by Hutus in Rwanda during a hundred-day period in 1994 is among the most egregious of these instances, resulting in the murder of 800,000 people.[150] Other such disasters include rebellions in the Democratic Republic of the Congo,[151] the suffering caused by an oppressive and incompetent regime in Zimbabwe,[152] massive human rights violations in Burundi,[153] and the huge toll inflicted on refugees in the Darfur region of Sudan.[154] Even when interventions on humanitarian grounds did take place in the post-Charter period, they were undertaken after considerable suffering and casualties had already occurred.

Preventive Cyber Attacks

States increasingly rely on cyber networks in managing their critical infrastructure. Attacks on these networks, including those of national security agencies, have become frequent. Defensive measures can successfully prevent most cyber attacks from causing damage, especially those launched by amateurs. But increasingly sophisticated attacks by States and others make clear that a fortress model of cyber security is untenable.

Cyber attacks can have substantial consequences. States that rely on cyber technologies to operate their critical infrastructure systems, such as power, transportation, and health, are vulnerable to cyber attacks regardless of their defensive capabilities. Successful attacks have the potential to cause deaths, injuries, and other damage comparable to major conventional attacks. Attacks aimed at Internet-based communications have disrupted government and commercial operations and caused significant economic harm. In April 2007, for example, coordinated attacks by clandestine groups on Estonia's banking system and government Web sites, during a dispute with Russia over natural gas supplies and prices, inflicted substantial economic damage.[155] In August 2008, during Russia's invasion of Georgia, cyber attacks on Web sites shut down virtually all Internet activity, forcing the Georgian government to use servers in Ukraine to continue its cyber operations.[156] The cost of defending against cyber attacks in the United States is estimated by the FBI at $66,930,950 in 2007, up from $52,494,290 in 2006, despite fewer companies responding to a survey.[157] Intelligence Director Michael McConnell said on January 16, 2009, "Cyber security is the soft underbelly of this country." He feared less that information will be stolen, than that networks will be destroyed, "causing a debilitating effect on the country."[158]

States are widely believed to be developing new capacities to prevent cyber attacks, but little is known about preventive actions in the past, or plans for the future. Laws against damaging cyber activities appear to apply to private individuals and companies, not to government actions. Transnational cyber activities are presumably subject to international law, but are essentially unregulated.[159] States are shaping policies on cyber attacks with little if any public disclosure or debate. The U.S. Defense Department recently formed a Cyber Command as part of the Strategic Defense Command, in order to develop and deploy a variety of defensive and offensive capacities. But it has provided few details, particularly concerning whether offensive cyber capacities might be used for preventive (or other) purposes in the absence of armed conflict.[160] Discussion about preventive cyber actions is therefore necessarily limited to public information and the nature of cyber technology.

The legality and legitimacy of preventive cyber attacks is likely to depend on the same general rules applicable to kinetic (physical) attacks, at least insofar as cyber attacks have comparable physical consequences. If cyber capacities are used to deal with kinetic threats, this analytic structure works well. But the rules are far less useful when contemplating preventive actions against cyber attacks. It is likely to be impossible, for example, for a State to know soon enough to permit preventive action whether a cyber attack is imminent, from where it is being launched, or by whom. Cyber attacks are commonly launched through computers and servers deliberately chosen to avoid disclosing the attacker's identity. It usually takes a considerable amount of time for even the most competent investigators to learn the source of a cyber attack, and it is often impossible to know precisely who is responsible or whether a State has authorized or supported the activity. These characteristics in turn limit the ability of States to deter cyber attacks by individuals or States, since they make retaliation unlikely. The types of preventive cyber actions that are potentially available as a technological matter is another factor that distinguishes cyber from kinetic operations. Once a cyber threat is identified, action can be taken against the locus of control of that threat, but such actions may fail to reach the ultimate source of the possible attack, and may cause unexpected consequences. States are likely, moreover, to regard preventive actions of this sort—where they have a physical impact and disrupt communications and controls over critical systems—as attacks on their territory.

The possible resort by the United States to offensive cyber attacks led the National Research Council of the National Academies to appoint a Committee on Offensive Information Warfare to examine the technological, policy, legal, and ethical issues involved. The report distinguishes between cyber and kinetic attacks, explaining that, among other factors, weapons for cyber attack are easier to use with high degrees of anonymity and plausible deniability, and are more uncertain in the outcomes they produce, making it difficult to estimate intended and collateral damage. While the Report concludes that the availability of cyber attack technologies for national purposes greatly expands the range of options available to policy makers in the United States and other States, it finds the existing policy and legal framework for guiding and regulating the use of cyber attack, given its potential direct and indirect consequences, "ill-formed, undeveloped, and highly uncertain."

The Report's principal recommendations reflect both the potential need for resorting to preventive cyber attacks and the dangers of doing so, by emphasizing the importance of establishing the proper framework for making decisions regarding such actions:

> 1. The United States should establish a public national policy regarding cyber attack for all sectors of government, including but not necessarily limited to the Departments of Defense, State, Homeland Security, Treasury, and Commerce; the intelligence community; and law enforcement. The senior leadership of these organizations should be involved in formulating this national policy.
>
> 2. The U.S. government should conduct a broad, unclassified national debate and discussion about cyber attack policy, ensuring that all parties—particularly Congress, the professional military, and the intelligence agencies—are involved in discussions and are familiar with the issues.
>
> 3. The U.S. government should work to find common ground with other nations regarding cyber attack. Such common ground should include better mutual understanding regarding various national views of cyber attack, as well as measures to promote transparency and confidence building.[161]

To the extent that States give priority to the secrecy of their cyber activities, serious international cooperation seems improbable. All forms of military activity are conducted with some degree of secrecy, but kinetic actions, even when undertaken in secret, are far more likely than cyber operations to be observed and reliably attributed.

Cyber attacks to prevent harm may sometimes be necessary and reasonable, even when the adversary is not known, because of the ability to discern conduct inconsistent with peaceful intentions. But unless measures are taken to ensure that such cyber attacks are acknowledged by the States that undertake or authorize them, it will be difficult if not impossible to establish their legality or legitimacy.[162]

Preventive War

States have launched "preventive" wars at various points in history, sometimes with no immediate defensive purpose. During the post-UN Charter period, as noted above, the United States considered preventive wars against the Soviet Union and China to prevent them from acquiring nuclear weapons, but decided against such attacks. Israel twice began wars against Egypt: in 1956, in response to terrorist attacks, and in 1967, in response to the massing of troops and other signs of an imminent strike by Arab forces. In 1973, Israel decided against acting preventively when Egypt massed forces at the Suez Canal, and as a result suffered a major attack that it was able to repel only after sustaining substantial casualties.

The attack on Iraq in 2003 by a coalition led by the United States is, in some respects, an example of a preventive war. Iraq posed no immediate threat to the States involved in the attack. The strategic rationale for the war was that the Saddam Hussein regime developed and was hiding WMD it was likely to use or provide to terrorist organizations, given his record of aggression and irrational behavior. The legal rationale for the attack was not, however, prevention, but rather enforcement of sixteen Security Council resolutions. The United States and its allies argued that resolutions dating back to the Gulf War of 1991 authorized the use of force, because Iraq failed to abide by them and ignored warnings implying that force would be used to enforce the Council's orders. This position was vigorously opposed by other members of the Security Council and is not accepted by most international legal authorities.[163]

CONCLUSION

The many categories of preventive force engaged in by States during the post-Charter period illustrate why prevention is a pervasive aspect of national and international security. They also demonstrate that the utility, legality, and legitimacy of uses of preventive force must be appraised by considering the context and form of each action. Uses of preventive force in national law enforcement, during armed conflicts, and in international waters are in principle lawful if they meet established prerequisites. States have significantly increased their reliance on preventive actions in national law enforcement. Other uses of preventive force have significant legal support or legitimacy even though they occur in foreign territory, such as efforts to rescue hostages or to stop gross violations of human rights. Still others take place despite their lack of legal support, for the purpose of protecting nationals, to enforce international principles or national laws in foreign States, and to prevent terrorist attacks that are non-imminent but likely. These types of actions are often viewed suspiciously or condemned by the international community, even when undertaken to suppress terrorist conduct that is illegal and that should have been prevented by the territorial State. Nonetheless, they continue to take place, and have in some instances met with at least muted acceptance.

The types of preventive actions vary in the amount of force involved, the threat being prevented, and the evidence available to judge the likelihood of the threat's realization. An abduction or targeted killing almost always requires less force than, for example, a rescue operation or an attack on a terrorist facility. In the former cases, moreover, the individual abducted or targeted has usually done (or is believed to have done) something concrete. A rescue operation necessarily implies, for example, that a State's nationals have been illegally seized. Justification for attacking a terrorist facility may be based on prior attacks by a group that has trained there, or solely on the prospect that some dangerous capacity will be developed. In all these situations the State considering force wants to prevent some form of damage, but significant differences exist in the amount of force needed and in the evidence supporting the preventive action.

In general, States rely on limited uses of preventive force more often than on major uses, no doubt in part because the latter entail greater risks. Limited uses of force are more likely to be tolerated by the international community than those with severe consequences or that last for long periods. Furthermore, even major threats do not necessarily require major uses of force to be thwarted; a limited use of force can sometimes prevent or deter a significant threat. Major uses of force for preventive purposes do occur, however, and are subject to the same risks of cost and difficulty as any war. The U.S. decisions to forego preventive wars against the Soviet Union and China are now regarded as eminently sound, in that neither of those potentially costly wars appears to have been necessary. The decision to depose Saddam Hussein, on the other hand, is widely questioned retrospectively as unnecessary, costly, and still possibly destined to fail. The same may be said of NATO's action in Afghanistan, despite its approval by the Security Council. The decision to forego a major preventive effort may, however, also end up being considered a costly mistake. Israel misjudged Egypt's intentions in 1973, enabling Egyptian forces to move deeply into the Sinai before being stopped at the cost of 5,000 Israeli lives and many more casualties. Decisions to forego even relatively minor uses of force may have grave consequences, as in the U.S. decision to withdraw from Somalia after the deaths of twenty-four U.S. Marines, and the decision thereafter by the United States and the Security Council to do nothing while 800,000 people were murdered in Rwanda.

No specific formula or rules appear to exist that can be used to predict international reaction to uses of preventive force that lack Security Council approval and fail to meet the ICJ definition of self-defense. While major uses of force are more closely examined than minor uses, how the international community reacts is likely to turn on factors related to legitimacy rather than on the specific legal categories into which the uses of force fall. Uses of preventive force that secure international support tend to be those that are necessary to address conduct internationally condemned or universally regarded as improper, and which are limited in scope and duration. Uses of force that appear unnecessary or which are not appropriately limited in scope and duration, but rather appear designed to advance a State's self-interest, tend to be regarded suspiciously, even when proper objectives are present.

CHAPTER FIVE

Dangers and Limitations of Using Preventive Force

The potential consequences of relying on force to prevent threats vary with the type of preventive action undertaken and its context. As was discussed in Chapter 4, preventive force in national law enforcement and during armed conflict is widely accepted as lawful and legitimate within parameters such as constraints on the use of excessive or improper force. However, these familiar issues differ from the issues that arise when preventive force is undertaken against another State, or against non-state actors within another State without its consent. Moreover, the potential consequences of using preventive force will differ depending on the extent of force, its purpose, and the strength of the evidence supporting it, including findings and mandates issued by the Security Council or other bodies.

Any transnational use of force presents dangers and limitations. Even an acknowledged, lawful, and legitimate use of force in self-defense, or one approved by the Security Council, may have serious adverse consequences. States have often decided against exercising their right of self-defense after an attack (as the United States did after the bombing of Pan Am flight 103). They may decide against seeking Security Council authorization to use force (Rwanda 1994) or enforcing such authorization (Gulf War 1991), due to possible adverse effects. Virtually every use of force, preventive or otherwise, entails dangers and costs that must be weighed against the potential benefits.

Preventive uses of force, in general, pose even greater dangers and potentially adverse consequences than uses of force in self-defense. This does not mean, however, that the optimal outcome will be assured in each case by deciding not to use preventive force. Each situation in which a genuine need exists poses simultaneously the inherent uncertainties that an action may be unnecessary to prevent an attack and that the failure to use force preventively will allow an attack (or other harmful consequence) to occur. Either decision—to act or to refrain from acting—may be wrong. Minimizing the probability of error depends upon having accurate information and exercising good judgment. The costs of each type of error depend on the consequences of acting versus not acting in particular cases. But whether a particular decision is correct, or less injurious than the other, will seldom be certain even in retrospect. No general rule is available to ensure foolproof decisions.

THE DECISION DILEMMA

In dealing with a threat, a government might face the choice of using force or not using it.

- *Either choice poses two potential errors:*
  1. That of a **False Positive**, acting in the erroneous belief that a real threat exists that can be prevented by using force; or
  2. That of a **False Negative**, failing to act in the erroneous belief that the threat is not real or cannot be prevented by using force.

- *Recent U.S. experience illustrates both types of errors:*
  1. Attacking Iraq in 2003 in the belief that it had WMD was a **False Positive** error. Iraq was found not to have such weapons; and
  2. Failing to use force effectively against Al Qaeda before its attack on September 11, 2001, was a **False Negative** error in that the U.S. underestimated the threat or the need to prevent it.

Many factors enter into each decision whether to use preventive force. Among the most important are: the estimated efficacy of further diplomatic efforts or sanctions, the potential effectiveness of military action, and the magnitude of the threat if left unaddressed by force.

Despite this inherent uncertainty, any responsible decision to use force—even if it is the only possible way to prevent a particular threat from being realized—must take into account that threatening or using preventive force may increase rather than reduce risk, or may fail to provide the protection sought.

ENHANCED INSTABILITY

A decision to make preventive force part of a State's declared national security strategy could deter potential target States and non-state actors from developing or using dangerous capacities, or from engaging in threatening conduct.[1] But adopting such a policy could also cause States or non-state actors to respond by announcing their own intention to use force first. Similarly, while the threat of preventive force may lead some States to give up WMD programs, such threats may cause other States to expedite such programs in order to deter threatened preventive action. Concrete threats of preventive force can, moreover, make any balance of destructive capacity that exists between the States involved more difficult or impossible to maintain.

UNCERTAINTY OF CONCLUSIONS

Decisions to use preventive force are based on predictions of future conduct of a State or non-state actor, and may therefore be more prone to error than decisions to use force in response to actual or imminent attacks. The extent of uncertainty is lessened when there is reliable evidence, as in the case of a hostage-taking or an existing humanitarian crisis. But, however reliable the evidence or intelligence used in concluding that the use of preventive force is necessary, it cannot be known with certainty that the attack or violation of human rights would in fact have occurred had preventive force not been used. A hostile regime or leadership may, for example, be forced from power before it acts, or may alter its policies for reasons other than its fear of a preventive attack. It is unrealistic to assume, moreover, that any State can be confident that it is capable of collecting and correctly appraising the evidence required to evaluate danger accurately, to identify critical targets, or to be certain that the threat involved can be entirely eliminated.

Decisions to initiate preventive action entail substantial uncertainties due to incomplete or incorrect information. These uncertainties will sometimes result in attacks that are based on error or inaccurate prediction, not only with regard to the intentions of the State or non-state actor that is attacked, but also with regard to the specific targets chosen.[2] Erroneous attacks and other forms of accidental damage frequently occur in law enforcement operations and armed conflict. But the use of force in a preventive context will be particularly susceptible to objections.

PROVOKING RESPONSE

A major danger in threatening or using preventive force is the response it can provoke from the targeted State or non-state actor. Victims of preventive attacks, undertaken without Security Council approval, are likely to have credible claims that they have the right to respond in self-defense. Preventive attacks are also more likely than responsive actions to generate resentment among nationals of the State that is attacked, and among sympathizers of non-state actors. Adverse public reactions, especially when fueled by noncombatant casualties, can undermine efforts to win support from such populations. Any use of preventive force must also take into account the capacity of the State or non-state actors attacked. Attacking the Taliban in Pakistan, for example, may have led to increased attacks, not only in Afghanistan, but also against the Pakistan government and other secular targets.[3] North Korea could respond to an attack on its nuclear facilities by attacking South Korea. President Eisenhower concluded that the United States could not successfully cope with Russian resistance even after a successful preventive war, rendering any such action inherently futile.[4]

The danger of an anticipated response to preventive force may, moreover, lead a State intent on such action to attack prematurely before a threat is fully developed, or with force sufficient to eliminate not only the particular threat but also the potential response. These tendencies will exacerbate the result of errors when they occur. Where the State attacked is believed to possess WMD, a preventive use of force would demand reliable and specific intelligence that ensures confidence that the threat will be neutralized with a high likelihood of zero counterstrike capability. Absent such intelligence, the decision to use preventive force may carry with it the need to use a level of force to ensure success that may be disproportionate or counterproductive.

LIMITS TO DETERRENT VALUE

The threat or use of preventive force against States may have considerable deterrent value, in that States are generally assumed to act in a calculated manner based on their interests. In some cases, the credible threat of preventive force may dissuade a State from pursuing a course of action or cause it to modify its intentions without altering its capabilities. Rational State actors will also be unlikely to provide WMD to organizations over which they have little or no control, if such conduct could lead threatened States to take preventive actions. On the other hand, a State threatened by an act of preventive force might seek covert partnerships with non-state entities as an asymmetric means of achieving its goals. For instance, a radical regime whose position might be internally weakened by a preventive strike, or which is threatened with being overthrown internally by liberal forces, could provide WMD (especially biological and chemical weapons) to terrorist groups whose use of them could exacerbate international tensions and help the regime to stay in power. Some regimes may, moreover, perceive their interests in irrational ways.

The threat or use of preventive force against non-state entities has less potential deterrent value than in the case of States, since such groups are not responsible for territory and population. States are assumed to endure indefinitely, and they make commitments to other States to secure reciprocal advantages. Most non-state entities lack these characteristics and incentives. Some deterrent effect may be secured by holding States responsible for activities of non-state actors within their territories. But even the defeat of a governing party such as the Taliban for supporting a non-state terrorist group will not necessarily ensure that the defeated party or the terrorist group it supported will cease efforts to inflict harm and to resume control.

LIMITED VALUE OF PREVENTION
BASED ON NATURE OF THREAT

Preventive force may be ineffective as a means for dealing with certain types of threats. For example, once a biological weapon has been developed, it may be impossible to neutralize that capability by force due to the ease of replicating and dispersing biological agents. To neutralize a biological weapon may require destroying the group that possesses it, which may be impossible or require the use of indiscriminate or excessive force. Nuclear-weapons programs are expensive, difficult to conceal or replicate in secret, and produce weapons likely to be traceable to the originator when employed. Biological and chemical weapons, on the other hand, are relatively inexpensive, can be produced with little or no external footprint, and once developed are more readily replicated, used, or transferred to others in secret.[5] Correctly identifying BW and CW facilities is also difficult because the same facilities are used for lawful production of biological and chemical products. These characteristics reduce the potential value of military strikes on BW or CW facilities, which in addition may lead to the release of harmful materials into the population.

Effective action with regard to BW and CW is therefore more likely through defensive than offensive measures, including stockpiling vaccines, antibiotics,[6] and masks, deploying sensors developed for detecting low levels of B/CW agents,[7] and supporting first-responder preparations.[8] Such defensive preparations may even serve a preventive function by indicating to a possible aggressor that a State has established the capacity to sustain itself by minimizing the consequences of such attacks, and thus will be able to respond.

INEQUITABLE APPLICATION

The costs of using force to prevent threats escalate with the power and capacities of the target States or non-state actors. The United States opposed Soviet interventions in Hungary and Czechoslovakia, for example, but did not use force to prevent them. No State or combination of States would likely even consider acting to prevent, for example, inhumane military action by Russia in Chechnya, or by China in Tibet, or controversial interrogation practices by the United States. Preventive force is therefore criticized as being reserved exclusively for use by strong States against relatively weak States and non-state actors. This result may be the consequence of political realities, without necessarily establishing that the use of preventive force where practical is any less legal or legitimate. Nonetheless, the inequitable application of force naturally tends to generate suspicions about its legality or legitimacy.

CAUSING MORE HARM THAN GOOD

A pervasive concern regarding preventive force expressed by experienced diplomats, political leaders, and security professionals is that it often does more harm than good. However real the benefits may appear, as is especially true in humanitarian crises, the actual results of intervening are often unpredictable and sometimes on balance deleterious.[9] Efforts to prevent harm through force may be poorly prepared or inadequately implemented, and may be unsuccessful in the long run even if they seem initially to produce positive results. No assurance exists, moreover, that a given use of force will be supported with adequate resources and political will for long enough to achieve success. The difficulty of achieving just results in some situations may be great, and interventions where ethnic divisions are strong may be exacerbated if seen as unfairly intended to protect one side in a conflict. Where actions are taken without proper legal justification, however necessary they appear, the principles of sovereign independence and territorial integrity tend to be undermined, arguably leading ill-motivated States and non-state actors to pay even less respect to these principles.

CHAPTER SIX

International Law and Preventive Force

The UN Charter is a treaty and its ratifying States are bound by its terms. The Charter governs the legality of uses of force. It provides that Member States "shall refrain in their international relations from the threat or use of force against the territorial integrity or political independence of any state, or in any other manner inconsistent with the Purposes of the United Nations" (Article 2(4)). This provision has been read by the ICJ and most international law scholars as prohibiting all threats or uses of force other than those approved by the Security Council under Chapter 7 of the Charter or that qualify under Article 51 as acts of self-defense against armed attacks.

These rules were reaffirmed by the High-level Panel report (pages 63–64), which found no need to modify them, since the Security Council is adequately empowered to deal with current threats through the use of preventive force or other means. The report recognized, however, that the Council often fails to authorize the use of force to curb conduct that threatens international peace and security. Some Member States oppose virtually any reliance on sanctions or force by the Council; some question the Council's authority in general; and most if not all ultimately act in their national interests, which often leads at least one Permanent Member to oppose authorizing force every time it is proposed, however necessary its use.[1] The

Council's frequent inaction accounts in part for the use of force by States without Council approval. Any practical evaluation of the use of preventive force therefore demands consideration of whether the ICJ's legal standards are viable as the exclusive basis for determining the propriety of preventive actions, and whether supplementary or alternative standards are available for that purpose.

SECURITY COUNCIL AUTHORITY

The Security Council has the power to approve uses of force, including uses of preventive force, once it determines that a situation constitutes a threat to "international peace and security" under Chapter 7 of the Charter. This power is indeed broad enough in principle to enable the Council to deal with most if not all the current threats that could potentially justify resorting to preventive actions. The only legal limitations on the Council's authority appear to be (a) the Charter allocation to individual States of "matters which are essentially within the domestic jurisdiction of any state . . ." (Article 2(7)), and (b) the argument that the Council cannot act in a manner that limits the "inherent" right of self-defense. Neither of these grounds has been given any restrictive effect in practice.[2]

The Council's authority is limited as a practical matter, however, by the power of each of its five Permanent Members to veto any non-procedural proposal. The end of the Cold War made it easier to overcome this limitation; the Security Council since 1990 has approved uses of force in connection with humanitarian crises (Somalia, Bosnia), in response to aggression (Iraq/Kuwait), and to combat terrorism (Afghanistan). The Council's authorization of troops for Macedonia was expressly characterized as "preventive" and has been treated as a new category of peacekeeping operations.[3] Council approval nonetheless remains a formidable obstacle; since 1990, the Council has failed to authorize force to stop egregious violations of human rights (Rwanda, Kosovo) and to enforce its own resolutions regarding North Korea, Iran, Iraq, and Sudan, among others.

Obtaining Security Council approval for preventive force is likely to be particularly difficult. Consensus on preventive actions will be possible only to the extent that consensus exists on the threat. The high standards of proof needed to gain the Council's acceptance may rarely be attainable within the time constraints such actions sometimes require, especially after the erroneous judgments made concerning Iraq's possession of WMD. It is also impractical to expect States to seek (or obtain) Council approval of some types of preventive actions, for example abductions and targeted killings. Even when the need for preventive action is established, the views and national interests of individual Member States will often undermine efforts to respond collectively.

The High-level Panel report urges that all States and regional organizations adhere to the view that Security Council approval should be *sought* for all uses of force other than those in self-defense against an actual or imminent armed attack. The report concludes (page 63), somewhat ambiguously, "that if there are good arguments for preventive military action, with good evidence to support them, they should be put to the Security Council, which can authorize such action if it chooses to. If it does not so choose, there will be, by definition, time to pursue other strategies, including persuasion, negotiation, deterrence and containment—and to visit again the military option." This statement can be construed to recognize, as a practical if not legal matter, that States may legitimately need to use force in situations where the Council will not approve its use. Assuming such an interpretation, the Report requires, at a minimum, genuine efforts to secure Council approval and the exhaustion of all alternatives before taking preventive actions without Council approval.

The United States and most major powers do not regard Security Council approval as an absolute prerequisite to the use of force even for actions other than self-defense, including humanitarian interventions. The United States in both the 2002 and 2006 National Security Strategy reports, as in all prior declarations of policy on the issue, reserves the option to use force without Security Council approval.[4] Foreign diplomats and national security experts in general understand (even if they do not accept) this position. Foreign participants in the Task Force's meetings were clearly upset, however, by the fact that the U.S. NSS reports do not discuss the Security Council's role in maintaining international peace and security. At no point do these reports acknowledge an obligation even to *seek* Security Council approval for uses of force when possible.

The EU Strategy, by contrast, states (page 9) that the "Security Council has the primary responsibility for the maintenance of international peace and security," a clause derived from Article 7 of the North Atlantic Treaty. The EU Strategy also states, however, that Europe is committed to "upholding and developing International Law," and that international organizations should be "effective in confronting threats to international peace and security, and must therefore be ready to act when their rules are broken."[5] This language suggests that the Security Council may be considered to have the "primary" responsibility for international peace and security without having the "sole" or exclusive authority. That appears to be the position of NATO, though individual European states that are members of NATO are divided,[6] with some declaring that the Council has the exclusive responsibility in this regard.[7] The African Union has a similar position, recognizing that the Council has the "primary" role in international security, but providing for the use of force without Council approval where authorized by the AU on any of the grounds specified in the OAU Charter.[8]

Latin American and Asian States are, in general, opposed to the use of force without Council approval, other than in self-defense as strictly construed. The Charter for the Organization of American States absolutely prohibits the use of force by one Member State in the territory of another.[9] Many Asian States claim to oppose the use of force in principle, and therefore almost always oppose reliance on sanctions or the use of force, even when authorized by the Council, especially with regard to matters having little or no transnational impact. Some insist that the Council lacks power to authorize the use of force in situations that are primarily domestic in character.[10]

Relying on the Security Council as the body primarily responsible for international peace and security is more likely to be meaningful now than during the Cold War. The Council has adopted principles and policies consistent with those supported by the United States and its allies regarding the three threats of greatest current concern: terrorism, human rights violations, and WMD proliferation.[11] Moreover, former Secretary General Kofi Annan and other world leaders have sought to enhance the Council's willingness and ability to act promptly and effectively to preserve international peace and security by calling for increases in UN capacities related to the use of force.

The High-level Panel report called upon the Council to confirm through an interpretive resolution the situations in which it will give serious consideration to authorizing the use of force to protect international peace and security; the situations identified by the Panel represent the same threats identified by the United States in both the 2002NSS and 2006NSS.[12] The Council failed, however, to respond to Annan's request. Even if an increased likelihood exists that resort to the Council will prove worthwhile in dealing with current threats, therefore, the Council may fail to respond effectively even when it has recognized the legitimacy of a particular objective.

The General Assembly (GA), though not a law-making body under the UN Charter, has at times lent crucial support to efforts by the international community to deal with threats to security. Where the GA acts unanimously or with near unanimity its resolutions have substantial weight. In the Uniting for Peace resolution of 1950 the GA resolved that it would deal with threats to international peace and security when the Council was unable to do so because of its lack of agreement.[13] In other resolutions the GA condemned apartheid in South Africa.[14] Increased emphasis on the potential role of the GA has developed as a result of these and other contributions to international security, and also due to the failure of efforts to expand Security Council membership to include Asian, African, and South American States.[15] The limited role assigned by the Charter to the GA, however, and the difficulty of obtaining near unanimity of support for policies from its Members makes it an unlikely source of consistent leadership.

SELF-DEFENSE

The UN Charter deals with self-defense in Article 51, which provides: "Nothing in the present Charter shall impair the inherent right of individual or collective self-defense if an armed attack occurs against a Member of the United Nations, until the Security Council has taken measures necessary to maintain international peace and security." Although this provision characterizes the "right" involved as "inherent" and states that "nothing" in the Charter shall be read to impair the right thus recognized, international law has in general developed in a manner that purports to limit the right of self-defense to actions taken in response to actual or imminent attacks.

In addition, the ICJ and international lawyers have advanced numerous other limitations on the right to self-defense. Some scholars argue (and the ICJ has recently so stated in an advisory opinion) that, to justify acts as self-defense, an attack must be by the forces of a State; attacks by non-state actors, including terrorist groups, do not qualify.[16] The ICJ has also narrowed the right of self-defense to attacks that are substantial, thereby forcing States that are subject to lesser attacks to rely on "other measures" to defend themselves (excluding, for example, collective action).[17] This suggests support for the argument that an "attack" on a Member of the United Nations must take the form of an attack on the Member's territory (with perhaps exceptions for embassies and troops). The ICJ has also made clear that a State may not invoke the right of self-defense in response to attacks by non-state forces from within a foreign State, unless the actions of the non-state actors are attributable to the State from which they have attacked; the victim State in such a situation is limited to using "proportionate measures," a concept with no established basis in international law and as yet undefined by the ICJ itself.[18] Another argument advanced is that defensive actions must cease once the attack involved is reported to the Security Council and it assumes jurisdiction, even though the measures taken by the Council may be insufficient to restore the Member attacked to full control over its territory and population.[19] If such narrow views of authority under Article 51 were treated as authoritative, self-defense would be unavailable, for example, as a basis for responding to the threats posed by terrorist groups, or to justify rescues of hostages in foreign territory, or for acting collectively with allies against state-sponsored assistance to subversive organizations.[20]

Regarding anticipatory force, the reading given Article 51 by international lawyers and the ICJ would not allow, and many have claimed it does not allow, any use of force in self-defense until an attack actually begins.[21] The High-level Panel report concludes, however, that international law does allow the use of preemptive force once an attack is "imminent," making it impossible to seek Security Council approval in advance.[22] This doctrine has wide support but rests on language so restrictive as to preclude almost any conceivable use of anticipatory force. The traditional rule, still quoted as authoritative, requires "a necessity of self-defense, instant, overwhelming, leaving no choice of means, and no moment for deliberation." Secretary of State Daniel Webster used this language in 1841 to describe when a State is entitled to use force to suppress efforts by insurgents operating from within another State, where the other State is both willing and able to suppress those forces.[23] He otherwise agreed in his 1841 statement that the propriety of anticipatory force should be evaluated by the general test of its reasonability under the circumstances.[24] In the post-Charter period, however, Webster's words have been used to describe the full scope of anticipatory self-defense. This reading leaves no room for preventive actions without Council approval for the purpose of averting any non-imminent danger, however serious the threat and however high the likelihood of its being realized. It also precludes lawful action to deal with any non-imminent threat posed by a group in another State, however unwilling or unable the foreign State may be to deal effectively with the threat.

The United States and other States have rejected some of the limits imposed by the ICJ on the right of self-defense.[25] Most States have disregarded them in practice, as the many instances of such actions in Chapter 4 reflect. The 2002NSS explicitly rejects the limitation that preventive actions may only be taken under threat of an "imminent" attack as restrictively defined, because (it concludes) the nature of current threats has made that understanding of "imminence" unworkable for dealing with grave threats likely to occur but at uncertain times and places. The document announcing the 2002NSS states (page 2): "as a matter of common sense and self-defense, America will act against such emerging threats before they are fully formed." The European Security Strategy is less supportive of preventive action but suggests (page 7) a need for change from "our traditional concept of self-defense," noting that the threat of invasion has been replaced by "new threats" which are abroad and dynamic.[26] Some security experts and scholars who accept as legally correct the restrictive use-of-force rules supported by the ICJ have nonetheless concluded that those rules are inadequate to deal with modern necessities arising from terrorism and humanitarian crises.[27] The widespread disregard of current use-of-force rules lends credence to these views and has led officials and scholars to propose alternative approaches to more accurately reflect current needs and/ or accepted State practice.

ALTERNATIVE APPROACHES TO USE-OF-FORCE RESTRICTIONS

At least four possible approaches have been adopted by States, or suggested by practitioners or scholars, in response to what they regard as the inadequacies of use-of-force restrictions. One approach, supported by those seeking to maintain the narrowest possible authority for uses of force not approved by the Security Council, is to recognize particular, limited exceptions where established rules prove unworkable. A second approach, officially advanced by the United States and supported by other practice and scholarship, is to read the Charter to permit uses of force consistent with its purposes and with the inherent right of self-defense as historically recognized by international law. A third approach is to use (implicitly if not explicitly) the concept of legitimacy as the standard by which to judge the propriety of uses of force, rather than relying on current legal standards. Finally, some national security practitioners and scholars advocate the view that uses of force are not susceptible to legal or moral standards, but rather reflect judgments made by States as to whether such actions are in their interests.

Recognizing Exceptions

A common response among international lawyers to the inadequacies of current use-of-force rules has been to create (or de facto recognize) exceptions for specific situations. Many international law scholars argue that, while it may sometimes be necessary in extraordinary situations to recognize that a violation of use-of-force rules was justifiable, such cases should be treated as exceptions in which illegal conduct is excused for overriding considerations, rather than as a basis for a rule that could be cited as authority in other cases, however analogous. NATO's use of force concerning Kosovo, for example, was widely regarded as both "just" and "necessary," but few scholars were prepared to approve the action as "legal."[28]

Critics of this approach find it untenable to both approve a particular use of force and at the same time refuse to acknowledge its legal propriety, including the right to rely on it as precedent in evaluating future uses of force. They are prepared to accept some exceptions to use-of-force rules as legally justified and generally applicable. The most widely proposed exception is that States should be recognized as acting lawfully when they use force, even without Security Council approval, to protect populations from grave and widespread violations of human rights. Another proposed exception would recognize the right of States to use force against non-state actors who engage in illegal attacks on their nationals or within their territory where the State in which the non-state actors are located is unwilling or unable to prevent such attacks. A third proposed exception would expand the concept of "imminence" to include situations in which an attack is highly likely but its precise time and place are unknown. These proposed exceptions illustrate how international law could adjust to enable States to deal lawfully with some current threats to security; none of them seems likely in the near future, however, to be accepted by the ICJ or other authoritative international law institutions as modifications of current doctrine.

Humanitarian Intervention The proposed exclusion for humanitarian intervention would, if adopted, constitute a significant exception to current use-of-force rules. Civil wars and other conflicts during the post-Charter period have resulted in the deaths of millions of civilians, often deliberately targeted on the basis of race or ethnicity.[29] Established norms of sovereignty, non-intervention, and self-determination accounted in the past for the lack of international legal authority to prevent these massive deprivations of human rights.[30] But as the international community developed new norms for the protection of individuals, reflected in the virtually universal acceptance of the Genocide Convention and other human rights treaties, the notion that States are obliged to protect their nationals from gross violations of such rights has become widely accepted. The UN Security Council, relying in part on these developments, expanded the meaning of "threat to international peace and security" to include humanitarian crises that are purely domestic in their immediate impact, and this expansion of authority has been broadly (although not universally) accepted by States and scholars.[31] The Council has been inconsistent in exercising this authority, however, having failed to act not only to avoid confrontations with its own Permanent Members, but also due to a lack of will—or uncertainty that it could act effectively—in the face of humanitarian crises in Rwanda, Burundi, Congo, Bosnia, East Timor, and Sudan, among other places.

The Council's anticipated unwillingness to approve using force to prevent the expulsion of Muslims from Kosovo led NATO to act without its approval. Most international law experts regarded this action as illegal, though legitimate and therefore excusable; but in their view Security Council approval continues to be a prerequisite for any lawful humanitarian intervention.[32] In his report to the General Assembly in 2000, Secretary General Annan called for an international consensus on a "responsibility to protect,"[33] which led the Canadian government to establish The International Commission on Intervention and State Sovereignty. The Commission released a report called "The Responsibility to Protect" (now abbreviated as "R2P") in December 2001, requiring that "every effort be made to encourage the Security Council to exercise—and not abdicate—its responsibility to protect. This means, as Article 24 of the Charter requires, prompt and effective engagement by the Council when matters of international peace and security are directly at issue. And it means clear and responsible leadership by the Council especially when significant loss of human life is occurring or is threatened, even though there may be no direct or imminent threat to international peace and security in the strict sense."[34] The High-level Panel report endorsed "the emerging norm that there is a collective international responsibility to protect." It agreed that this is a moral responsibility, not a duty, and is "exercisable by the Security Council authorizing military intervention as a last resort, in the event of genocide and other large-scale killing, ethnic cleansing, or serious violation of international humanitarian law which sovereign Governments have proved powerless or unwilling to prevent."[35] Subsequent resolutions have confirmed these principles, and "R2P" is currently an accepted doctrine recognizing the Security Council's authority to intervene in such situations and the responsibility of individual States to work to prevent such atrocities within the limits of that restrictive view of the Charter.

Some States and many scholars have urged that international law recognize in principle that proper humanitarian actions are lawful, even when undertaken without Security Council approval. They argue that humanitarian intervention differs from uses of force for other purposes, in that humanitarian interventions are always consistent with the Charter's most fundamental purpose—protecting human beings from gross violations of their rights. Such interventions are justified, they urge, when undertaken on the basis of solid evidence, after all other alternatives are exhausted, and after a variety of prerequisites are established, such as the lack of any improper motive by the intervening State or States.[36]

These and other arguments for making humanitarian intervention lawful have failed to establish the legality of humanitarian interventions that lack Security Council approval, in part because the distinction between humanitarian and other purposes is difficult to maintain. Humanitarian claims can be fabricated or exaggerated, and are usually accompanied by other, self-interested motivations. NATO's action in Kosovo, while undoubtedly intended to prevent a humanitarian disaster, was also motivated by the desire of NATO countries to avoid being forced to absorb a huge outflow of refugees. Some of the most positive humanitarian results have been achieved through interventions undertaken primarily, if not exclusively, for non-humanitarian purposes. For example, Tanzania removed the racist murderer Idi Amin from power in Uganda to prevent him from continuing attacks on Tanzanian territory that were expected though not imminent. Vietnam removed the genocidal Pol Pot regime from power in Cambodia in response to its own strategic concerns about the regime's close ties to China.

Nor is it clear that preventing serious humanitarian violations is in all instances a more valid purpose under the Charter than preventing non-humanitarian threats, such as a devastating terrorist attack. Though the need for preventing humanitarian violations is often clearly established before force is used, the need for other types of interventions is sometimes equally clear before force is contemplated, as when hostages are taken or a series of suicide bombings has taken place. All forms of preventive action are, moreover, predictions of future events that may turn out to be inaccurate. Humanitarian interventions, like other preventive actions, may turn out to have been unnecessary, prove unsuccessful, or be far more costly than the benefits they confer. The effects of military actions, whatever their purpose, are essentially the same, with casualties, economic damage, violations of human rights by soldiers, and other unintended but harmful consequences.[37] These considerations have led even strong advocates of humanitarian intervention to refrain from advocating that they be recognized as a separate legal basis for States to use force.

Preventing Terrorist Attacks The argument for recognizing preventive actions aimed at terrorists as legal relies on the fact that terrorist attacks can be as damaging as conventional ones, and that the States from which terrorists operate are duty-bound to prevent them from attacking people and targets in other States. The Security Council expressly declared that the attacks of September 11, 2001 gave rise to the right of self-defense, and it has issued a detailed list of duties that States have regarding terrorist groups. The ICJ has ruled, however, that the right of self-defense exists only after an attack by a State's military forces, or by groups controlled or sent by a State's government.[38] Under current law, therefore, a State's failure to prevent attacks by a non-state group on foreign territory provides no basis for the use of force within its borders against either the State or the group itself. Apart from Security Council approval, the victim State in such situations is limited to using what the ICJ has described as "proportionate measures," an ill-defined concept that appears intended to allow actions necessary to exclude the non-state actors from the State's territory.[39]

Revising the Concept of Imminence An interpretation supported by the United Kingdom, the United States, and respected scholars would allow greater flexibility in exercising anticipatory force by revising the concept of "imminence" to reflect current threats. The U.K. Foreign Ministry's Legal Advisor suggested treating as an "imminent" threat of attack any situation in which a terrorist group that has already engaged in attacks retains the capacity and intent to do so, "even if there is no specific evidence of where such an attack will take place or of the precise nature of the attack."[40] This rationale would cover situations in which a State or group has established that it is a threat, for example, by conducting a prior attack, and has the means and propensity to inflict harm, but where it is impossible to know when the attack might occur. To the extent this rationale applies only to situations analogous to an ongoing conflict, it adds no new authority but makes clear that the threat of an attack by any hostile group that has already demonstrated its hostility may be regarded as "imminent." If the rationale were applied to situations in which the State or group has established itself as a genuine threat, this approach would create significant legal flexibility along with the dangers of error and abuse.

Charter-based "Reasonable" Uses of Force

Another approach for dealing with the inadequacy of current use-of-force rules is to construe the Charter to provide greater flexibility than current rules allow. This approach deals with the claim that Article 2(4) prohibits all uses of force other than in self-defense by distinguishing between uses of force consistent with Charter purposes and the territorial integrity of States, on the one hand, and uses of force inconsistent with those principles, on the other.[41] This approach also views the right of self-defense as having been preserved in its historical entirety by Article 51, allowing all uses of force in self-defense that are reasonable under the circumstances.[42] Virtually every U.S. administration since President Truman has on one issue or another advanced arguments for flexible use-of-force standards. Several administrations, including Kennedy, Johnson, Reagan, Bush, and Clinton, have in official statements described the proper approach to the use of force as a multi-factored analysis aimed at determining the reasonability of uses of force based in part on the provisions and purposes of the Charter.[43]

A more flexible approach to the use of force, based on the Charter's purposes and on reasonableness, has significant support in the domestic laws of states (where force is frequently regulated by rules based on legislative purpose and reasonableness). Political leaders and national security practitioners are naturally inclined to evaluate and justify uses of force on the basis of all factors that are relevant to a particular situation.[44] An approach based on reasonableness would, for example, evaluate proposed uses of preventive force based on the gravity of the danger, the likelihood of its realization, the exhaustion of other means for prevention, the extent to which UN Charter-based procedures and values support the action, and the proportionality of the action contemplated relative to the danger perceived. From its very beginnings, international law recognized the prevention of harm as "the first just cause of war," allowing defensive measures that are "necessary" in the light of an enemy's power and intentions.[45] Supporters believe an approach based on the consideration of all relevant factors would be useful as a principled and transparent basis for evaluating uses of preventive force.[46]

The ICJ and most international lawyers reject basing the legality of using force on the Charter's purposes or reasonableness. They regard the Charter's language as unambiguously restricting uses of force to those approved by the Security Council or in self-defense against armed attacks. They recognize that State practice has gone beyond these limits, but believe that allowing Charter-based or "reasonable" uses of force in self-defense would leave too much discretion to States to determine unilaterally their right to use force in the absence of an actual or imminent armed attack.

Proponents of the historical reasonableness test argue that States prepared to ignore the law will be no more likely to do so with a flexible rule than if they are governed by relatively inflexible, mechanical rules. States determined to ignore the law have in the past advanced flagrantly unjustifiable positions. (For example, Germany, Japan, and Italy claimed before World War II that they were acting in self-defense when they invaded, respectively, Poland, Manchuria, and Ethiopia.[47]) Proponents of the reasonableness test believe, moreover, that use-of-force standards reflecting real-world considerations would tend to cause responsible States and national security practitioners to examine the relevant factors more systematically, and thereby to minimize mistakes. The ICJ, however, and most international law scholars find the reasonableness standard too flexible, too subjective, and open to abuse by powerful States.[48]

Legitimacy as a Substitute for Legality

The widespread acceptance by States of unauthorized uses of force in circumstances inconsistent with impractical legal rules has led some to suggest abandoning those rules in favor of an approach based on legitimacy. While this idea is primarily advanced as a basis for evaluating the propriety of humanitarian interventions, the rationale is applicable to other preventive uses of force. Advocates contend that legitimacy provides a more widely accepted and effective vehicle than current legal rules for establishing guiding principles.

Supporters of the current restrictive rules of international law are reluctant even to consider articulating standards to guide States in situations where the Security Council fails to deal with a genuine threat. The Dutch Advisory Committee on International Law, while conceding that "one cannot close one's eyes to the possibility" that the Security Council may fail to act where it might reasonably be expected to do so, nevertheless does not "believe there is any point, before such a situation arises, in designing a set of criteria for an emergency of this type that would make military action permissible or even desirable."[49] Providing such guidance would, at least in cases not involving "massive violations of fundamental human rights," run the danger of "giving an unintended impression of legitimating such military action in advance." Providing such advice in advance was "scarcely possible" in any event, since "legitimacy requires not only action in accordance with predefined principles and decision-making based on agreed procedures, but also widespread international support for the outcome."

The High-level Panel approved a different position on this question. It accepted the need for a multi-factored analysis in determining the legitimacy of force, recommending that the Council adopt "a set of agreed guidelines, going directly not to whether force can legally be used but whether, as a matter of good conscience and good sense, it should be." It proposed "five basic criteria of legitimacy: (a) Seriousness of threat . . . (b) Proper purpose . . . (c) Last resort . . . (d) Proportional means . . . [and] (e) Balance of consequences."[50] (Report at 67). The report states, however, that its proposal for establishing guidelines to evaluate the legitimacy of uses of force is intended for situations where the use of force would be lawful by traditional standards. The report fails to explain, though, why it included among the factors that it believes establish legitimacy some of the factors necessary to establish legality. If legitimacy is strictly a supplemental test beyond legality, the legality-related guidelines would already have been considered before the legitimacy question arose.

While the High-level Panel may not have intended legitimacy guidelines to become an alternative to strict legality, that could be the practical result of its proposal. It is difficult to imagine, for example, what uses of force that meet the test of legitimacy proposed by the High-level Panel should not be undertaken because they are not actions in "self-defense" as strictly applied, or had not been approved by the Council. Furthermore, if the legitimacy guidelines proposed by the High-level Panel are satisfied in a particular case, it is similarly difficult to explain why such a record should be considered insufficient to justify the use of force in other, indistinguishable cases. Nonetheless, while legitimacy may serve as a practical substitute for legal standards in some cases, it is highly unlikely to be accepted as such by established international legal institutions.

Force Based on National Interest

A common response among national security practitioners to the inadequacy of traditional use-of-force rules is to ignore the rules and engage instead in an interests-based calculation. Some governments and commentators think U.S. officials regard themselves as exempt from the traditional rules by virtue of the primacy of U.S. military and economic power. Justifications for this broad discretionary power over the use of force include the arguments that the United States is the most likely target for many potential aggressors, and that it should use its influence and power to lead the world in advancing objectives such as freedom and human rights, rather than be bound by rules intended to support politically neutral outcomes.[51] This approach would leave the United States largely unbound by rules in determining whether to exercise preventive force, although subject to the realities and risks accompanying unilateral military initiatives.

Some may contend that this approach provides the most accurate description of how States actually behave. Yet, few if any States would agree with the legality or legitimacy of so broad an allocation of authority to any other State. No U.S. administration since the Charter's adoption has officially asserted such a prerogative. To the extent such authority is claimed by any State, other States could advance reciprocal claims, potentially increasing international instability. It seems clear, moreover, that so broad a claim of authority is unnecessary to provide adequate security from threats potentially requiring the use of preventive force.

CONCLUSION

International law severely constrains the use of preventive force. The only forms of anticipatory force regarded as legal under currently accepted rules are those approved by the Security Council or in self-defense as narrowly defined by the International Court of Justice. While these limits are widely disregarded in practice, none of the alternative legal standards for evaluating uses of force is likely to take the place of the current rules. Instead, States and regional security organizations appear to be using force on an ad hoc basis in response to threats. The legal rules have been left in place as formally authoritative norms,[52] while State practice has diverged on important issues, in the absence of any widely accepted, systematic set of standards that could potentially enhance both security and consistency.

CHAPTER SEVEN

Legitimacy and Preventive Force

The concept of "legitimacy" has no established place in the United Nations Charter. Legitimacy is also a word used in many different contexts, and with differing meanings. It has been used synonymously with morality, justice, and legality, among other ideas. Any effort to advance a meaning of "legitimacy" that purports to rationalize all uses of the word in evaluating international behavior would be futile. It is therefore a difficult concept to apply as a standard of conduct.

Yet, legitimacy is widely relied upon by States, diplomats, national security practitioners, and scholars in evaluating international uses of force. As the High-level Panel on Threats, Challenges and Change concluded, the concept is useful in appraising the propriety of uses of force, however much weight one gives to current international law standards. The frequent disregard of legal standards in practice, however, and their ineffectiveness in regulating State conduct with regard to the most serious current threats, have led to the use of legitimacy as a supplement or substitute for strict legality. What the Danish Institute for International Affairs wrote concerning humanitarian intervention applies as well to other situations widely felt to require preventive actions: "[I]t is hardly realistic in the foreseeable future that states should altogether refrain from such intervention if it is deemed imperative on moral and political grounds."[1] Participants in conferences held by the Stanford Task Force on Preventive Force repeatedly cited the importance of establishing the legitimacy of uses of force, and of avoiding actions likely to be viewed as illegitimate. If preventive force is to have any place in national security strategy, its use should be based on standards and procedures designed to enhance its legitimacy.

As used in the High-level Panel report, "legitimacy" is meant to convey both a general principle for evaluating uses of force that differs from strict legality and a method by which this general principle should be implemented based on objective criteria. The general principle conveyed by this use of "legitimacy" is that it represents the anticipated reaction of the relevant international community to a State's decision to use force—including preventive force—and it prescribes that a State should take into account those reactions before acting, rather than relying exclusively on its own view. An inquiry into legitimacy is necessarily one, therefore, by which a State considers the opinions of others, even if it is not bound to abide by those opinions.

This general observation has several components, reflecting both legitimacy's complexity and its potential power. To begin with, legitimacy is by definition to be derived from the actual views and values of States and other relevant parties concerning proposed or actual uses of force, rather than solely the views of international lawyers about specific provisions of the Charter. Accepted and practiced legal standards are relevant, but so are other norms and values. The use of force by indigenous groups to end colonial rule in several places is nowhere authorized by the Charter but nonetheless gained almost universal acceptance, often even among the colonial powers themselves. Other uses of force that cannot be justified under strict legal principles may widely be regarded as legitimate, including preventing gross violations of human rights, rescuing hostages, protecting nationals, or attacking individual terrorists.

Conversely, the legality of an action does not itself necessarily establish its legitimacy. Just as a State seeking to be guided by legitimacy in resorting to force may look beyond legality to the opinions of others, a State seeking to establish the illegitimacy of a use of force within its territory must also look beyond legality to the opinions of others. Serbia argued emphatically, for example, that NATO's bombing to stop it from expelling Muslim Kosovars was illegal, as the action was neither approved by the Council nor justifiable as self-defense. But even an illegally invaded State may fail to establish the invasion's illegitimacy when it has engaged in conduct universally regarded as a fundamental violation of human rights. The Security Council can establish the legality of any use of force under international law by approving it in a resolution. But its decisions may not always represent what is legitimate. The Council's resolution blocking both Serbs and their Muslim victims from obtaining arms was widely viewed, for example, as illegitimate, as it allowed the well-armed Serbs to massacre Muslims without meaningful resistance; and the prohibition was disregarded by many States as a result. Legitimacy forces an evaluation of each action based on its underlying merits, beyond strict legality. No single entity can unilaterally determine legitimacy, however established its legal authority or power.

Another aspect of this general understanding of legitimacy that distinguishes it from legality is that it usually takes the form of a relative judgment, rather than a definitively positive or negative one. By its nature, the concept of legitimacy is one that turns on numerous factors given differing weights in particular situations by varied players. Legality, on the other hand, demands that certain standards be met regardless of many factors considered in determining legitimacy, leading to a clear conclusion. Given the variety of players whose views are relevant to legitimacy, moreover, and their divergent interests, significant uses of force are unlikely to be universally viewed as legitimate or illegitimate. The mere fact that powerful states have more to gain than weak ones from resorting to force will influence each group's views on the legitimacy of such actions. Legal rules governing the use of force, on the other hand, are deliberately intended to eliminate discretion in their application by purporting to establish bright lines applicable to all States. Furthermore, legitimacy is a dynamic concept, based on standards and views that may change. Legality is based on established rules, and international lawyers generally insist on a static view of the Charter's limits on the use of force, demanding definitive evidence of changes in practice before recognizing emerging norms and standards.[2]

A major difficulty in relying on the concept of legitimacy is determining how to measure the positions of States and relevant organizations and individuals. At the United Nations, each Member State has one vote in the General Assembly, but in the Security Council only fifteen Members may vote, and only the five Permanent Members may exercise the veto. Legality is established by the Council's approval, but legitimacy could not be based solely upon a method that always gives such disproportionate weight to the votes of particular States. An overwhelming vote in favor or against some action in the General Assembly, on the other hand, may have no legal force under the Charter, but has considerable weight in determining legitimacy. As noted by the High-level Panel report (page 48): "[T]here is particular value in achieving a consensus definition with the General Assembly, given its unique legitimacy in normative terms." Taking into account the views of all States does not, however, require that equal weight be given to each State's official position. Legitimacy necessarily entails considering each State's interest in a matter and the merits of its position. Credibility is important in judging the weight that should be accorded positions advanced by the State that acts and by States that vote or comment on the action's propriety. States with reputations for illegitimate conduct will have that burden to overcome. States aligned with the State using force will normally be assumed to be biased in the latter's favor, while those aligned with the State against which force is used (or which may be adversely affected) will be assumed to be biased against the acting State. Important evidence can nonetheless develop in such situations. A State may oppose its ally's action, or a State expected to oppose an action may join in its support. Preventive actions undertaken without the support of traditional allies will tend to be viewed with greater skepticism by other States.

An evaluation based on legitimacy must take into account, moreover, not only the views of States, but also those of international agencies, regional organizations, non-governmental groups, the press, the public, religious leaders, and influential individuals. The weight these positions are given will depend on such factors as how strongly they are held, and the influence, reputation, and objectivity of the entity or individual expressing them. Evaluations of legitimacy are ultimately based on the aggregate impression of the views of all relevant actors regarding a proposed or implemented action. Where a general consensus exists that a preventive action was appropriate, it enjoys a high degree of legitimacy. Significantly, the absence of strong criticism of a use of force may itself provide the action some legitimacy, whereas such evidence would be given little weight in an evaluation of its legality.

Of particular importance in establishing an action's legitimacy is the need to avoid both the reality and the perception that the action was taken to advance inappropriate objectives. Preventive actions that result in material benefits to the State that uses force are especially prone to condemnation. Efforts to control territory, resources, or the political makeup of a government will tend to undermine claims of legitimacy, even if other appropriate objectives are present. The U.S.-led coalition's action in Iraq, for example, may have secured greater support if the coalition had not assumed sovereign control of that State, an unprecedented measure in the post-Charter period, and one that lent support to claims that the United States planned to exploit Iraq's oil resources,[3] Vietnam's action in Cambodia in

1978–79 ended the rule of a murderous regime, but was nonetheless considered illegitimate by most UN Member States because Vietnam exercised control over Cambodia's territory and policies for longer than necessary to accomplish its legitimate objectives.

Testing the legitimacy of an action is worthwhile, despite the complexity and uncertainty of the judgments required. The High-level Panel explained (page 53) that "the effectiveness of the global collective security system, as with any other legal order, depends ultimately not only on the legality of decisions but also on the common perception of their legitimacy." Domestic security systems rely heavily on laws and have enforcement mechanisms, including police forces and courts, to compel compliance even with rules that lack public support. In the international arena, however, it is often legitimacy, not law, which explains why States adhere to rules and standards of conduct despite the absence of enforcement mechanisms. Legitimacy, therefore, is as important a measure as legality for judging the appropriateness of State conduct, as its proper application reflects considerations that actually lead States to abide by international rules and norms. This reality gives legitimacy other advantages. The legitimacy of a particular use of preventive force can affect the cost and difficulty of the action, due to the higher level of financial support, active participation, and acceptance it can secure. This in turn will affect the likelihood of an action's success and the durability of its outcomes. An action's illegitimacy, on the other hand, will tend to increase its costs and decrease its likelihood of success and the durability of its outcomes, reflecting the opposition and active resistance that illegitimacy tends to generate. Even legal actions that lack legitimacy will tend to be more costly and ineffective than those viewed as legitimate. Legitimacy does not ensure success, but enhances its prospects.

Implementing a policy of testing possible uses of force for their legitimacy requires more than a commitment in principle. Legitimacy is made effective when implemented as a guide to conduct through a disciplined process of evaluating an action in light of accepted standards of conduct and potential reactions from the international community. Considerable resistance exists in the international community to developing standards and procedures as guides for the proper use of preventive force for humanitarian or other purposes. Some contend that such efforts are likely to be self-serving and subjective, and could increase the tendency of major powers to use force by justifying interventions against weaker States.[4] Refusing to identify the factors that establish or undermine the legitimacy of preventive uses of force cannot, however, diminish their existence and influence. Applying such criteria, on the other hand, should guide States considering preventive force and thereby lead to fewer, more limited actions for proper purposes, rather than more frequent, less justifiable ones.

Several studies and scholars have advanced criteria by which unauthorized interventions should be evaluated. Differences of opinion are inevitable. But the differences are less significant than the extent of agreement as to the relevant factors, if not their content. The High-level Panel report, for example, cited five criteria to apply in conducting such an evaluation (pages 53–54): "(a) Seriousness of threat . . . (b) Proper purpose . . . (c) Last resort . . . (d) Proportional means . . . [and] (e) Balance of consequences." These criteria have long been established in international law and practice, and are commonly used in judging the conduct of States. Other studies and scholars propose somewhat different standards.[5] This chapter discusses these and other standards, and in addition proposes measures to enhance their effective implementation. In doing so, it considers how these standards and other measures might apply to situations likely to arise as a result of current threats to security, including potential attacks by non-state actors from States incapable or unwilling to prevent such attacks; the acquisition of WMD by States considered likely to use them illegally or to provide them to non-state actors; and humanitarian interventions.

STANDARDS UPON WHICH LEGITIMACY DEPENDS

Seriousness of Threat

The High-level Panel report identifies the seriousness of a perceived threat as the first factor to weigh in evaluating the legitimacy of preventive force. The report suggests that threats that are not clearly established and serious will lack legitimacy: "Is the threatened harm to State or human security of a kind, and sufficiently clear and serious, to justify prima facie the use of military force?" The Report also suggests that internal threats may satisfy this criterion, where the harm anticipated is grave: "In the case of internal threats, does it involve genocide and other large-scale killing, ethnic cleansing or serious violations of international humanitarian law, actual or imminently apprehended?" (Report, Paragraph 207(a)).

In general, a demanding standard should be applied to justify preventive actions not approved by the Security Council.[6] Threats cited by the United States and other States are described as potentially serious enough to justify preventive action. But consideration of the three situations noted above illustrates the important differences and specific questions likely to arise depending on which threat is at issue.

Terrorist actions aimed at civilians are by their nature potentially serious. The fact that a single person or small group may be the source of a particular threat does not necessarily mean the threat is not serious. That judgment would turn on the capacity of such individuals or groups and on whether they are associated with a larger entity or movement intent upon and capable of doing substantial harm. Also highly relevant will be the extent to which the State in which the non-state actors are located could be relied upon to make a preventive action unnecessary. Where the government of the State involved supports the terrorist group, as in the case of the Taliban's support for Al Qaeda, the danger posed by the non-state actors is likely to be far greater than where the government has not assisted them, and even more so when it is attempting to prevent illegal conduct. The danger posed by a non-state group independent of the State in which it is located depends on the State's capacity and willingness to prevent attacks by that group. Necessity in such situations will generally be established only if a well-intentioned State cannot take effective preventive action.

Proliferation of WMD is seen by many security professionals as the greatest danger posed by State or non-state actors. WMD in the hands of a radical non-state group such as Al Qaeda may be the greatest danger of all. As a general rule, the danger will depend on the record of conduct by the acquiring State or group. States led by governments that have attacked other States illegally, especially if they used WMD, will reasonably be seen as particularly dangerous. The fact that a State has violated international commitments under the NPT or Security Council resolutions in acquiring or proliferating WMD would undermine the reliability of its other commitments. States that have supported terrorist groups with conventional weapons, or assisted in the proliferation of WMD, may reasonably be seen as likely to share WMD with such groups.

Humanitarian interventions are rarely if ever made before a serious threat exists; usually they occur well after gross violations of human rights have taken place. Proponents of such interventions propose that they be undertaken only after "gross, persistent, and systematic" violations of human rights are underway or imminent.[7] Others suggest using the ICC Statute definitions of crimes against humanity to establish danger. Setting such rigid standards seems inconsistent with the concept of legitimacy, in that grave danger may reasonably be seen to exist in other situations. Many States, especially in Africa, feel that they need to prevent illegal takeovers of governments, because their leaders are very likely to create humanitarian crises after taking control. A military coup, for example, could signal grave dangers depending on whether its leaders have demonstrated a disregard for law and human rights.

Necessity ("Last Resort")

States have universally accepted the principle that uses of force can be legitimate only when necessary. The 2002NSS and 2006NSS make clear that diplomacy and all other feasible alternatives must be exhausted before resort to force. While this principle is well established, disagreements often arise in specific situations over whether force has become the measure of last resort. All credible options should be exhausted to enhance legitimacy, but account may be taken of special circumstances, such as the urgency to act.[8] Normally, economic or political sanctions should precede uses of force in all preventive situations, but some sanctions may be even more damaging to noncombatants than force.

The need to use force is likely to be established only after a clear warning has been given to the State or group posing the serious threat, and evidence that the State or group thus warned has refused or is unlikely to mitigate the danger. A government's or group's past failure to cease improper behavior in the face of UN resolutions or reasonable demands would lend support to the conclusion that force is necessary.

Necessity will also depend on the type of threat posed. Terrorist actions launched from foreign territory may fail to establish a need to use force if the foreign State is able and willing to step in. When a State is unable or unwilling to prevent attacks by non-state actors from its territory, despite having been asked to do so, or helps such an actor, the need to act without that State's cooperation should be seen as established. When a foreign State assists or directs a non-state group in conducting attacks in other States, the case for using force within and even against the former is particularly strong.

Efforts to reduce the threat from WMD proliferation before using force would include, for example, establishing effective means of verifying compliance with non-proliferation treaties and assuring the availability of nuclear fuel for peaceful purposes.[9] On the other hand, the need to act preventively may be satisfied where further delay would make force ineffectual, or make a much greater amount of force necessary, or cause significant damage that an earlier use of force would have avoided. Measures to establish necessity before a humanitarian intervention might include, in addition to warnings, the dispatch of observers or peacekeepers and creation of safe areas. A State's failure to cease or prevent human rights violations after a clear warning should, however, normally establish necessity.

Legitimacy also depends on limiting the amount of force to what is necessary. For this reason, among others, U.S. and European armed forces have shifted dramatically toward the use of precision-guided munitions, and increasingly rely where possible on non-lethal weapons. International law does not mandate using the most advanced, and least lethal, weapons in all cases. A general rule to that effect could discourage the development or deployment of such weapons. The concept of legitimacy makes relevant, however, not only whether a measure is legally required to meet the mandated standard of necessity, but also whether it can achieve the relevant military objective with less harm.

Proportional Means

A long-standing, universally accepted standard applied in evaluating uses of force is the principle that both the right to use force and the amount of force used should be proportional to the danger involved. Proportionality is a complex concept. Its meaning is often disputed. It is an indispensable element of legitimacy, however, because the extent to which it is disputed reflects the importance that is attributed to the interests it represents.[10] Treaties, legal decisions, and scholarship have provided useful guidance.

An action's legitimacy, even assuming the propriety of using force in principle, will depend on whether the amount of force used is proportionate to the danger to be averted. Excessive force is force that is unreasonable in light of its objective, its consequences (including impact on noncombatants), and the availability of less damaging means.[11] Treaties have outlawed biological, chemical, and certain other weapons on the grounds that their use is never justifiable. Most weapons are allowed, however, but their use must avoid "superfluous injury or unnecessary suffering," as well as "indiscriminate attacks."[12] Proportionality in this sense, like legitimacy in general, is not left solely to the unfettered discretion of combatants, but rather represents legally enforceable requirements that prohibit pointless or excessive damage to civilians or combatants.

The ICJ decision in *Nicaragua v. U.S.* suggests a "tit-for-tat" approach in defining proportionality, subjecting defensive measures to a "strict and objective" standard that asks whether they were necessary relative to the actions that justified response.[13] Whatever legal rule may govern this issue, legitimacy should not require responses in kind, but rather measures reasonably required to deal effectively with a threat. Furthermore, the proportionality of an action should depend on the overall evidence of the threat involved, not just on the action closest in time to the use of preventive force. The standard implicit in the High-level Panel report is consistent with these premises (Paragraph 207(c)): "Are the scale, duration and intensity of the proposed military action the minimum necessary to meet the threat in question?"

The proportionality of a preventive use of force requires particularly careful consideration, especially if no illegal act has yet occurred. The quarantine of Cuba, implemented during the Kennedy administration, is widely regarded as a properly calibrated preventive response to a grave threat that had not yet been manifested by any attack on the United States. While a major use of force may be necessary to prevent, for example, a dangerous State or non-state actor from acquiring WMD, it would nonetheless be impossible to justify as proportionate if its consequences included large-scale injury to noncombatants or other violations of the laws of war. Limitations on the conduct of military operations resulting from actual attacks should be applied with full force to military operations initiated for preventive purposes.

Satisfying the strict legal requirements of proportionality may be insufficient, moreover, to avoid widespread condemnation on legitimacy grounds. The force required to achieve a lawful objective may nonetheless be perceived as excessive. Here, as in other aspects of legitimacy, perceptions about a use of force can be as important as its legality. Actions that extend for long periods, or that severely harm noncombatants, will tend to be judged more harshly than those that are over quickly and are effectively targeted. Groups prepared to engage in terrorist acts frequently exploit these factors, deliberately using schools and other protected facilities as sanctuaries, depots, or bases for attacks. While the law may allow attacks against such facilities when improperly utilized, the challenge of establishing legitimacy will nonetheless require careful consideration of the human consequences.

International Support

The legitimacy (and effectiveness) of an effort to use force to prevent a threat is enhanced to the extent it has support from other States, especially through the Security Council.[14] This factor is in principle recognized by both the 2002NSS and 2006NSS, as well as the strategic doctrines of NATO and the European Union. African interventions for humanitarian purposes, and to restore democratically elected governments, have almost all taken place with the approval of regional organizations and within the territories of their members. An unsuccessful effort to secure the Council's approval is, where feasible, considered "an indispensable condition for the legitimacy of humanitarian interventions,"[15] and this view applies with equal if not greater force to interventions on other grounds. Where Council approval is not attainable, legitimacy is enhanced when States secure the broadest possible support in the General Assembly

and from regional organizations and individual States. The process
of seeking international support often reveals the opposition to an
intervention, which can be a valuable indicator of its ultimate legitimacy. Legitimacy may also be enhanced if the intervening State
reports on its actions to the Council and other interested international organizations. These reports provide evidence of the intervening State's purposes and activities, and enable the organizations to
provide their reactions, including their support.

Securing international support for uses of force, especially Security Council approval, not only enhances the legitimacy of preventive actions, it reduces the risk of error through debate and scrutiny.
In addition, international support increases the prospect that the
burden of approved military operations will be shared. The costs of
the 1991 Gulf War, legally authorized by the Security Council and
widely supported, were largely paid by States other than the United
States, although U.S. forces did most of the fighting. NATO's action
in Yugoslavia was viewed by many States as legitimate, though less
clearly legal than the 1991 Gulf War; States other than the United
States paid 60 percent of the costs and shared significantly in the
military burden. The U.S.-led action in Iraq commencing in 2003
had less international support than either the 1991 Gulf War or the
action in Yugoslavia, forcing the United States to bear almost all the
costs and most of the fighting. Finally, international support will
tend to establish that the motive for a preventive use of force goes beyond serving the national interests of the State asserting its necessity,
a particularly important factor in establishing legitimacy.

Some scholars consider at least some international support an
essential prerequisite to the legitimacy of humanitarian (and therefore presumably all other) interventions unauthorized by the Security Council.[16] This position gives a valid consideration undue
weight. While enhanced legitimacy is secured by a State in obtaining
international support for a preventive use of force of any type, an

absolute rule that treats as illegitimate every unauthorized preventive action would result in erroneous judgments in some cases. The circumstances of a particular case might leave a State no feasible option to secure the approval or support of even one additional State before acting preventively. A State may also have good reason for failing to secure support when, for example, no other State is prepared to approve or undertake the costs of preventing a particular humanitarian disaster.

Charter-based Objectives ("Proper Purpose")

The High-level Panel report (Paragraph 207(b)) identifies "proper purpose" as one of the criteria by which the legitimacy of uses of force should be tested: "Is it clear that the primary purpose of the proposed military action is to halt or avert the threat in question, whatever other purposes or motives may be involved?" The genuineness of a State's intentions in using preventive force will inevitably be weighed in the appraisal process. But an evaluation of proper purpose should begin by considering the type of threat and whether the international community, and the Security Council in particular, recognize it as reflecting a proper purpose under the UN Charter. This exercise will tend to test the purposes alleged to exist in each situation against relatively objective criteria. Charter provisions and several Security Council resolutions and widely adopted treaties establish as proper the purposes of preventing terrorist attacks, illegal proliferation of WMD, or gross violations of human rights, among the other current threats to security:

> • *Terrorism:* The Security Council and General Assembly have condemned all forms of support for terrorism and terrorist groups (e.g., Resolution 1373, September 28, 2001). Several widely adopted treaties (thirteen are appended to Resolution 1373) also make such support and many specific forms of conduct illegal. The threat or use of preventive force, therefore, gains legitimacy when used within a State

complicit in tolerating or supporting groups that use its territory as a base for terrorist operations, or against a group that violates terrorism conventions or rules regarding the protection of noncombatants.

• *WMD Development or Proliferation:* UN resolutions and several treaties make illegal the development, possession, use, and proliferation of some forms of WMD in certain circumstances.[17] Many States have agreed to additional constraints, particularly regarding nuclear weapons and technologies. The threat or use of preventive force gains legitimacy if invoked in connection with illegal weapons development or proliferation, especially such serious violations as the transfer of nuclear explosive material (plutonium-239 or uranium-235).

• *Deprivations of Human Rights:* Many treaties and resolutions make illegal certain grave deprivations of human rights, including genocide and torture.[18] Military actions for the purpose of protecting people from violations of established rights are likely to derive significant legitimacy from these norms. While international law provides no support for the proposition that a State can use force against another State in order to advance the political freedoms of the other State's nationals,[19] in Africa a clear relationship is seen by many States between the illegal overthrow of democratic governments and the widespread deprivation in those countries of human rights. African States, acting through ECOWAS, SDEC, and the AU, have used force on several occasions to restore illegally removed democratic regimes.[20]

In addition to those Charter purposes that are expressly reflected in resolutions and treaties, the legitimacy of a State's intervention will inevitably be affected by the extent to which it seeks to prevent conduct universally condemned in the laws of nation States. The Charter recognizes that, in formulating international law, consideration should be given to the standards adopted by States in their national laws.[21] National norms do not become international standards merely because they are universal. But the universal recognition of the inappropriateness of certain conduct, such as murder and theft, reflects underlying expectations that affect the judgments of States as to the propriety of preventing such conduct through international uses of force.

Some scholars have suggested that humanitarian interventions should be considered legitimate only when undertaken by States that "do not stand to gain either politically or economically from the intervention."[22] This standard for legitimacy seems both impractical and artificial. Even when the intervention involved is humanitarian, a State genuinely intending to stop a crime against humanity may also be interested, for example, in preventing an inflow of refugees across its borders. The High-level Panel implicitly recognizes that States that use force may have more than one purpose in doing so, suggesting only that the "primary" purpose be to prevent the threat in question. While this standard leaves open for debate whether an action is "primarily" for one purpose or another, it is more realistic than insisting that the State taking action be exclusively motivated by the purpose of halting the threat involved.[23] It may be more accurate, in fact, to conclude that, where a State intervening for some proper purpose genuinely intends to achieve that purpose, its other purposes should be considered irrelevant so long as they do not themselves violate Charter-based objectives. Some of the most important humanitarian interventions were motivated by purposes other than the desire to protect victims (Tanzania/Uganda; Vietnam/Cambodia; India/Bangladesh). Yet, preventing further harm to victims was genuinely intended and achieved in those situations, and the interventions were ultimately accepted by the international community.

On the other hand, any threat or use of preventive force is properly considered illegitimate if its purpose is inconsistent with Charter-based objectives, or with widely adopted treaties such as the Genocide Convention, or in universally accepted principles of conduct constituting customary international law. Preventive action to maintain strategic hegemony, for example, or to acquire the sovereign territory of another State, or to control the resources or government of another State for any longer than a proper purpose requires, would fail to reflect a proper, Charter-based objective.

The genuineness of a State's purpose in using force will be judged, not only by the existence of a threat that reflects an accepted Charter-based objective, but also by the extent to which its preventive action is shaped to achieve that purpose and no other, improper objective. Actions genuinely motivated by the protection of nationals, for example, may lose their legitimacy if conducted in a manner that reflects other, less appropriate purposes, such as replacement of a government. Scholars suggest, for example, that in an unauthorized humanitarian intervention "armed force is exclusively used for the limited purpose of stopping the atrocities and restoring respect for human rights, not for any goal going beyond this limited purpose."[24] It follows "that any unauthorised military intervention should be limited and once the goal is attained, the intervening forces should withdraw."[25] Although sound as general principles, these observations cannot be applied mechanically. At times, an intervention may be able to achieve its proper object only through removal of the government responsible for the threat or humanitarian crisis; and it will often be necessary to engage in some post-intervention reconstruction in order to increase the prospects of success, which is itself a standard by which the legitimacy of preventive interventions must be judged.

Confidence in Findings and Conclusions

Uses of force are always accompanied by uncertainties. Uses of preventive force are particularly prone to doubts, given that preventive actions often entail evaluating potential and uncertain threats. Some argue that preventive actions are inherently prone to error, due to the difficulty of predicting the future and the lack of reliable intelligence.[26] Developing reliable intelligence about non-state actors, such as terrorist groups, may be even more difficult than obtaining reliable evidence on the capacities and intentions of States. This conclusion would support the view that States may in general justifiably regard preventive actions as illegitimate. When a State faces a threat that it knows or reasonably perceives to be grave, however, the lack of intelligence sufficient to know when the threat will be realized may cause that State to rely even more on preventive action, or to adopt overwhelmingly destructive measures to ensure that the threat is eliminated. The legitimacy of actions in the face of uncertainty will be affected by the genuineness and gravity of the threat involved.

The cause of uncertainties that lead a State to consider using preventive force is also relevant to the legitimacy of doing so. A State may deliberately generate concern as to its intentions by adopting secret programs aimed at developing WMD or by deliberately misleading other States regarding its intentions. The 2006NSS notes (page 24) that "there will always be some uncertainty about the status of hidden programs since proliferators are often brutal regimes that go to great lengths to conceal their activities." It cites Saddam Hussein's ability to hide advanced WMD programs before the 1991 Gulf War and his strategy of "bluff, denial, and deception" prior to the 2003 intervention. It may be appropriate to deny a hostile and intransigent regime protection from preventive attack when it refuses to provide threatened States the information necessary to make reasoned judgments.

Also relevant to the legitimacy of a preventive action is whether the uncertainty regarding a threat concerns its timing rather than its seriousness or likelihood. The 2006NSS (page 23) refuses to "rule out the use of force before attacks occur, even if uncertainty remains as to the time and place of the enemy's attack." The legitimacy of using preventive force in such situations will depend on the reasonability of a State's conclusion that the threat it faces is grave and might occur suddenly, despite the lack of evidence sufficient to resolve such uncertainties as timing or specific targets.

It is wrong to assume, moreover, that preventive actions will almost always be made without sufficient intelligence. The extent and types of uncertainty decision-makers face in making preventive force decisions are likely to vary, and the level of proof necessary to justify a particular action will depend on the evidence actually available. Sometimes, evidence of the gravity of the threat and the likelihood of its taking place will be readily available. States should determine before using preventive force which relevant facts are known and whether the record permits a reliable judgment.

- In evaluating whether to use preventive force to target a suspected terrorist or group, for example, the uncertainties associated with such a decision will be reduced if the individual or group is known to be associated with Al Qaeda and to have engaged in terrorist acts. Even if the prior hostile acts of such an individual fail to satisfy the ICJ's requirements for invoking self-defense, their gravity—along with proof of the individual's or group's intentions—may nevertheless establish a strong case that another attack is probable.
- When the threat concerns proliferation of WMD and its potential use, any proof of illegal proliferation or testing, or the refusal to allow required inspections, may create justifiable concerns. A State may reasonably conclude that it faces an unacceptable threat when strong evidence exists that another State has illegally acquired WMD, even though it is uncertain whether that State will ever share such weapons with a non-state group likely to use them. The danger posed by such a situation will depend on the acquiring State's prior willingness to supply advanced weapons to such non-state groups, as well as its policies on sharing such weapons and its hostility toward the threatened State. In some situations, chaotic conditions that could lead to the overthrow by a radical group of a State that possesses WMD might justify preventive action.
- Similarly, the need to intervene to protect an ethnic group from grave violations of human rights may be established beyond any reasonable doubt when grave and systematic attacks are already taking place. Humanitarian interventions, like hostage rescues and some other forms of preventive force, typically take place after individuals at risk have been harmed and their safety is in jeopardy. The uncertainty that remains in such cases is only whether additional harm will be inflicted. Reports of peacekeeping forces, international agencies, and responsible NGOs will often reduce uncertainties regarding humanitarian threats.

Perhaps the most authoritative forms of evidence upon which a State may rely in evaluating the need for preventive action are the findings and conclusions issued by the Security Council and other international institutions regarding the existence, seriousness, and urgency of threats to international peace and security. The Council, for example, often makes findings of serious violations of international duties and human rights constituting a threat to peace and security, while failing nonetheless to authorize the use of force to prevent further harm. In such situations, a State may justifiably rely upon such findings and conclusions, even though some may ultimately turn out to be erroneous. This is particularly true when the State accused of destabilizing conduct fails to respond to the Council's demands. Such findings are generally made with care, and are regarded by the international community as conveying legitimacy. Findings and conclusions regarded as having been made without adequate care, or in a biased manner, will confer little if any legitimacy, however legally authoritative the issuing entity. Findings and conclusions based on evidence that is kept secret, moreover, are likely to be given less weight than those based on publicly available evidence.[27]

Much needs to be done to improve the care and competence with which intelligence related to use-of-force decisions is collected and used by States and the Security Council. Two commissions have recently examined the strengths and limitations of the U.S. intelligence community and the manner in which intelligence has been used in resolving uncertainties related to attacks on the United States and other foreign threats such as the existence of WMD in Iraq.[28] Among the principal conclusions of these commissions are these needs:

- Develop a culture in the intelligence community of "competitive analysis" to stringently test hypotheses.
- Identify and compare what is known and what is believed.
- Separate the functions of policy and analysis to prevent inappropriate influence of analysis by policy considerations.

- Rely on integrated, multi-source analysis, rather than single-source assessments.
  - Share information within and among all relevant agencies.
  - Limit protection of sources and methods to permit adequate discussion and evaluation.
  - Maintain a steady level of financial support for all aspects of intelligence operations to achieve consistently acceptable results.

These criteria and recommendations apply, not only to States, but also to intelligence evaluation by the Security Council and other international and regional organizations.

Balance of Consequences

The final standard cited by the High-level Panel report for evaluating an action's legitimacy is the principle that a careful weighing of the balance of consequences should precede every use of force. The High-level Panel report put this in the same way as it has historically been expounded (Paragraph 207(e)): "Is there a reasonable chance of the military action being successful in meeting the threat in question, with the consequences of action not likely to be worse than the consequences of inaction?" This overall question is an essential inquiry in testing the legitimacy of any use of force. A proposed action that is viewed as unlikely to overcome the threat in question, or as likely to cause more harm than good, should be considered illegitimate regardless of the merit of its objectives. The fact that an action is or would be viewed as likely to fail or to result in more harm than good may itself increase the likelihood and the costs of failure. Actions considered illegitimate on this ground, as on others, lose support and are met with greater resistance.

A State should exercise care in determining whether preventive force is likely to succeed in its purpose and do more good than harm. Estimating the consequences of uses of force is always hazardous and often impossible to accomplish with confidence. An erroneous judgment, even in good faith, will not alter the fact of failure or the harm inflicted, or the judgment of illegitimacy likely to follow. Actions undertaken unilaterally that fail or do more harm than good are especially likely to be condemned as illegitimate, regardless even of their legality.

Success, in the sense intended by this test, is not merely a matter of seeking international approval in advance by satisfying standards and procedures associated with legitimacy. It means actually succeeding in the use of force undertaken, and in a manner that avoids causing so much harm that the success is morally negated. This entails taking into account the dangers associated with preventive actions, described in Chapter 5. It also requires evaluating the specifics of each proposed intervention. The chance of success, and the prospect of doing more good than harm, will vary with the type and complexity of the action contemplated, the extent of force required, its duration, and the human and material costs.

Virtually any type of preventive attack will face the prospect of failure, or of causing more harm than good. Limited actions, such as hostage rescues or targeted killings, have failed or caused disproportionate costs, while actions with potentially grave consequences, such as attacks on WMD facilities, have succeeded with limited costs. In general, major actions that continue for long periods are more likely than limited, short-term actions to entail greater costs than benefits. On the other hand, limited actions that avoid dealing with the underlying causes of significant threats may in the long run cause far more harm than good. Nation-building and reconstruction are costly, but failing to engage in such activities where they are necessary to remedy the threat addressed may render any limited effort futile. These uncertainties are greatly heightened in situations where failure will predictably entail major costs, as in the case of attacks on States that possess WMD or capacities and resources that will enable them to respond to attacks with highly destructive actions.

Evaluating the benefits and harm of a preventive use of force should go beyond the immediate, physical effects of a particular action and take into account the long-term, ethical consequences. An action that has immediate success and saves lives in the short run may ultimately result in a high risk of failure and much higher casualties by creating lasting enmity and conflict. On the other hand, a particular effort that is expected to fail, with greater casualties than inaction would immediately entail, may be an appropriate step in a long-run, successful effort to resist an enemy that would otherwise be permitted to inflict harm on far more people over time.

MEASURES LIKELY TO AFFECT LEGITIMACY

The legitimacy of a threat or use of preventive force is likely to be enhanced if the State contemplating such an action adheres to procedures designed to make clear its need and justification. The credibility of a State's preventive action is likely to be advanced, moreover, by measures to establish the State's good faith. Limiting the preventive action's scope and duration to reflect its alleged proper purpose is particularly important in establishing good faith. The measures described below help make a case for legitimacy.

Report to Security Council

The UN Charter requires that all uses of force in self-defense be "immediately reported" to the Security Council (Article 51). Potential uses of preventive force are more likely to be accorded legitimacy when a report is made to the Security Council in advance of any military action than if no report is made. Such reports provide an opportunity for multilateral discussion of the threat perceived, of measures that could avert the threat short of the use of force, of possible Security Council approval of the use of preventive force to deal with the threat, and of other criteria related to legitimacy. A State's failure to make any report or to refuse to discuss and explain a use of force is given significant weight by the international community in considering the action's legitimacy.

Security Council or other multilateral review of the propriety and effects of a preventive use of force should continue after the action, or should be initiated by a report at that point if review was not possible in advance. Interventions gain legitimacy when retroactively approved by the Council or other body capable of conferring approval. Ongoing scrutiny by the Council or other presumptively neutral body will also tend to support an action's legitimacy. Post-action review provides a mechanism to monitor and influence the extent to which States that take preventive action limit appropriately the scope and duration of their activities.

Development of Multilateral Capacity

Former Secretary General Annan warned that States feel forced to act unilaterally in part because the UN Security Council lacks the ability to call upon dedicated forces to deal with threats promptly and effectively. To the extent the Security Council's lack of capacity and willingness to deal with threats can be remedied through measures such as those recommended by the High-level Panel, States will likely treat multilateral action through the Security Council as a more viable option.[29] The 2006NSS describes a strategy for dealing with regional conflicts that includes "conflict intervention," and concludes (page 16): "[T]he international community does not have enough high-quality military forces trained and capable of performing these peace operations." It calls for enhanced capacities at the United Nations and associated regional organizations "to stand up well-trained, rapidly deployable, sustainable military and gendarme units for peace operations" (page 45). Greater multilateral capacity to deal with threats will make such operations more likely to succeed, which will tend to enhance the legitimacy of such efforts. A State's willingness or unwillingness to support efforts to enable the Security Council to act effectively to prevent threats to international peace and security is likely to be taken into account by the international community in evaluating that State's decisions to act unilaterally.

Developing an Evidentiary Record

A State contemplating resort to preventive force should, if possible, first present the evidence it claims justifies such extraordinary action to the Security Council or other appropriate forum. The legitimacy of an action will depend significantly on the evidence available to support its necessity, and also on the effectiveness of a State's presentation of that evidence. Evidence purporting to establish a need to use preventive force should be subjected to stringent, public scrutiny to enhance the likelihood of accurate conclusions as to its reliability and significance. In addition, where such an effort is made, the Council or other entity considering the matter may be able to alleviate the need for preventive force by requiring the State whose conduct has generated serious concerns to respond to or remedy those concerns. Exhausting such a procedural opportunity will itself enhance the legitimacy of any action that follows, especially where the State whose conduct is at issue refuses to cooperate or fails to satisfy reasonable concerns as to its intentions.

Accountability

The legitimacy of preventive actions is enhanced when States undertaking them agree to be held accountable in some manner for the mistakes they make. Supporters of the legal rules currently governing the use of force have suggested holding States accountable for violating those rules through decisions of the ICJ or the International Criminal Court.[30] This suggestion in effect proposes treating the legitimacy of uses of force in the same manner as their legality. It is likely to be rejected by States that regard current use-of-force rules as too restrictive, but are prepared to consider the legitimacy of their conduct. Voluntary mechanisms of securing accountability, on the other hand, are appropriate methods for enhancing the legitimacy of preventive actions.

Many States expressly grant authority in treaties to the ICJ to review disputes with other States that potentially involve the use of force, and the ICJ has construed treaties implicitly to confer such authority.[31] Other States have refused, however, to authorize the ICJ to decide use-of-force disputes, or have revoked prior submissions to the ICJ's jurisdiction. Decisions of the ICJ, moreover, can be enforced only through resolutions of the Security Council. This limits their utility in holding States—especially Permanent Members of the Council—accountable for uses of force. The ICC can impose criminal liability on individuals it holds responsible for violations of the crimes contained in its Statute, including crimes against humanity or the laws of war. It may someday also assert jurisdiction over the crime of "aggression," thereby expanding its authority to hold individuals liable for illegal uses of force.[32] But several major States, including the United States, have refused to submit to the ICC's jurisdiction, and its prosecutor has not yet attempted to prosecute officials from non-Member States.[33]

More generally, it is unrealistic to expect States to agree to mechanisms for accountability that would enforce rules they regard as unacceptably restrictive. States that currently decline to accept ICJ rulings on use-of-force issues do so because they disagree with those rulings. A broader consensus exists with regard to the legal rules currently enforced by the ICC, but no such consensus is likely were the ICC to attempt to enforce use-of-force restrictions through criminal prosecutions.

A more likely approach to accountability would encourage States to adopt measures that cause them to exercise a higher degree of care in determining whether to use force. States that resort to preventive force should, for example, consider paying compensation for harm caused by errors of judgment or implementation. Procedures could be established to enable the Security Council to perform forensic examinations in such situations. To be credible, any such process must be structured to operate impartially and with authority to obtain relevant evidence. Other mechanisms for accountability may be possible for shifting the costs of improper uses of preventive force, including voluntary arbitration.

The United States and Israel have both indicated a willingness to apologize and pay compensation for damage caused by questionable uses of force, even in armed conflict. The U.S. Department of Defense established a Commander's Emergency Response Program in 2003, pursuant to which it agreed voluntarily to pay for the adverse consequences of certain actions taken in Iraq and Afghanistan.[34] On September 17, 2008, Secretary of Defense Gates was reported as having accepted an Afghan proposal to establish "a permanent joint investigative group to determine the facts surrounding civilian casualties more quickly. And he pledged that even before all the facts were known, the United States would apologize for civilian casualties and offer compensation to survivors."[35] Israel has apologized and paid compensation for deaths or injuries of Palestinian civilians resulting from targeted killings.[36] Such measures enhance legitimacy by tending to ensure that decisions to use force will be made with greater care than would be the case in the absence of such commitments.

The case for accountability in the form of damages caused by preventive force in the absence of armed conflict is even stronger than in situations such as Iraq, Afghanistan, and Gaza. Damages caused in armed conflict are presumed to be justifiable, and States are immune for conduct that satisfies the laws of war. Preventive actions carry no such presumption and international law provides them no such specific immunity where they lack any established legal basis. Furthermore, collateral damage caused by a preventive action may more likely be regarded as unwarranted than damage caused during armed conflict, given the relative lack of legal authority for preventive actions and the greater uncertainties they usually involve. Accountability therefore seems a useful measure for enhancing the legitimacy of preventive actions.

CHAPTER EIGHT

Conclusion

Contemporary threats pose grave dangers to national and international security, including terrorist attacks against civilian and economic targets, the proliferation of weapons of mass destruction, and massive deprivations of human rights. The potential harm from these threats has been dramatically demonstrated in attacks on the United States, culminating on September 11, 2001; by several subsequent attacks on civilian targets in other States; by the proliferation of WMD and missile technology; and by the continued racial, ethnic, and political murder and oppression of millions of human beings by their own governments.

Preventing the harm posed by these threats, and the potential devastation that could be caused if WMD reached the hands of irresponsible States or non-state actors, is in principle as desirable an outcome as preventing harm in other aspects of life. But the transnational use of force to prevent harm before its infliction is imminent entails substantial risks because of the inherent uncertainties associated with unrealized threats, the danger of erroneous or bad-faith claims or assessments, and the adverse responses likely to follow. Preventive force can exacerbate the very problems it is intended to alleviate by causing conflicts that may otherwise have been avoidable and by provoking or alienating States or groups possibly reachable through other measures.

This study responds to proposals by the U.S. government and others that, despite these risks, preventive force should be available in appropriate circumstances to deal with particularly dangerous contemporary threats. It treats as "preventive" those uses of force, unauthorized by the Security Council, that fail to meet the legal standard that permits "preemptive" force when the threat addressed is "imminent." It examines the extent to which preventive actions are undertaken by States, and the international community's reaction to them.

Preventive actions in the contexts of national law enforcement and armed conflict are generally regarded as an appropriate and effective method for dealing with threats of serious harm. States universally use domestic law enforcement measures that rely on force in various forms to prevent terrorist attacks, rather than merely punishing such conduct after the fact. Laws have been widely adopted that increase the capacity and authority of national law enforcement to prevent threatened harm through exclusion, detention, investigation, and arrests, not only for completed terrorist crimes but also for conspiring, aiding or abetting, financing, and, in some States, merely encouraging such crimes. And the preventive approach has had considerable success. Similarly, States engaged in armed conflict with other States or non-state groups routinely rely on force to prevent attacks, to reduce casualties, and to enhance the prospects of success in such engagements. Uses of force in domestic law enforcement and armed conflict must be necessary and reasonable, but no requirement exists in these contexts that force be used only in response to actual or imminent crimes or attacks.

Given the frequent use of preventive force by States to ensure their domestic security and in armed conflict, it should not be surprising that States sometimes use force to prevent transnational threats. But using force in another State's territory without consent violates its sovereignty and territorial integrity. The UN Charter has been construed to permit States to use force within the sovereign territory of other States only with the Security Council's explicit authorization, or in response to an actual or imminent armed attack. These limits are premised, however, on the assumption that States will perform their duties as sovereigns to refrain from illegal actions against other States and their own populations, and will seek to prevent terrorists from using their territories as sanctuaries. It also assumes that the Security Council will act to ensure international peace and security by authorizing the use of force in response to threats. Both assumptions are at times incorrect. States are therefore frequently faced with threats caused by the misconduct or failures of other States, and have to deal with them without Security Council support.

The result has been the repeated use of force by States in a variety of situations that fail to meet applicable legal standards. Many States used force, for example, without Security Council approval to end colonialism, and with broad support in the international community. Equally frequent, though less widely supported, were interventions by the Soviet Union and United States that attempted to subvert governments they opposed or to protect governments they supported. Actions have also been undertaken to prevent harm to nationals, to abduct individuals, to rescue hostages, and to kill persons for defensive and other reasons. Force has been used against terrorists and their facilities when the States in which they are located cannot or will not suppress their illegal activities. WMD facilities have been attacked and substantial military actions have been taken against governments to prevent them from oppressing their own nationals, or to remove them from power for illegally displacing democratically elected leaders.

States seem likely to continue to use preventive force in these and other situations, despite the fact that their actions are unauthorized by the Council and respond to threats that are non-imminent by traditional standards. Certain categories of actions will expand over time, while others diminish. But numerous, varied forms of preventive action seem inevitable so long as the Security Council remains divided on such issues as using force to prevent terrorism, nuclear proliferation, and humanitarian disasters. International reaction to these preventive actions will continue to differ, moreover, based not on their formal illegality, but rather on circumstances present in each case related to the justification for the action. Some actions will be formally condemned, and followed with sanctions and even the threat or use of force. Others will be opposed less emphatically, ignored, or approved tacitly or expressly despite being illegal.

The frequent disregard of the International Court of Justice's use-of-force rules has left States without credible guidance in considering whether to threaten or use force. This led the Task Force to consider whether certain legal positions should be modified to provide greater flexibility to States and regional organizations in enhancing security, in a manner consistent with Charter purposes. The notion, for example, that only a State can launch an "armed attack," thereby allowing resort to the right of self-defense, is a highly artificial reading of the Charter, inconsistent with the Security Council's resolution recognizing that Al Qaeda's attacks permitted the United States to engage in self-defense in Afghanistan. The meaning of "imminent" could also be adjusted to reflect the need to prevent highly probable and damaging terrorist attacks by known groups able to keep secret the specific time and place they plan to strike. Restrictive readings of the Charter such as these seem likely to be disregarded by many States in dealing with contemporary threats to security or humanitarian crises. Nonetheless, alternative legal approaches to use-of-force issues are unlikely to be accepted by the ICJ or most international lawyers. It seems futile, therefore, to expect changes in the relevant legal rules to provide a credible process for evaluating the propriety of preventive actions.

The High-level Panel on Threats, Challenges and Change recognized the need for better guidance for States on use-of-force issues. It insisted that international law should be maintained in its current form, and proposed Security Council reforms that might have enhanced its performance. It also proposed, however, that States should be guided by the concept of legitimacy in considering force, irrespective of their legal rights. The Task Force agrees that the concept of legitimacy provides the best available set of standards by which States that decide to use preventive force can enhance the likelihood of reaching responsible decisions acceptable to the international community.

The utility of considering the legitimacy of preventive actions stems from the principle that a State contemplating the threat or use of force should consider, not only its own view of the propriety of its conduct, but the views of others in the international community. Legitimacy is a complex idea that can mean many things, and it provides no clear judgments, one way or the other, based on a single factor such as the imminence of a threat or a particular State's legal responsibility for the actions of terrorists it fails to control. It is nonetheless a potentially useful method if implemented through a set of specific standards and procedural measures based on Charter values and actual practice. Thus applied, it requires systematic consideration of those factors and circumstances that experience has shown carry weight in the judgments of other States and the international community.

Legal rules purport to provide clear, authoritative guidance; but clear answers have little value if they fail to secure compliance because they prevent legitimate outcomes. Legitimacy provides no clear or absolute rules, but the standards by which legitimacy is established are based on the actual views of the relevant international community, and are therefore more likely to be effective at evoking conduct consistent with those views. A process that tends to result in outcomes that reflect the reactions of the international community seems clearly preferable to one that is limited to considering legal rules that are disregarded as impractical or inconsistent with current security needs and Charter purposes.

This report's survey of State practice provides examples of the considerations that appear to lead to positive and negative reactions to uses of force. Among the factors given weight in determining an action's acceptability are its size and duration, presumably because limited actions generally result in fewer casualties and reflect limited, more readily achievable objectives. The genuineness of an action's need, however, and the manner of its implementation seem particularly important concerns. The same type of action, for example, may receive different responses based on the need established in each case, and the correlation of the measures adopted in each instance with their claimed purpose. For example, an action demonstrably intended to capture a known terrorist in a State that is unwilling or unable to arrest him will receive greater support than the same type of action within a State that is able and genuinely attempting to satisfy its legal obligations. An action intended to protect nationals is likely to be accepted so long as it is fashioned to reflect that purpose and not used to displace a government the acting State opposes. A humanitarian intervention is more likely to be condoned where necessity is clear and no ulterior motive is at play.

This report has expanded on the High-level Panel's suggested standards for determining legitimacy, based on UN Charter purposes and established norms of conduct. These standards, and the procedural measures proposed, represent the most likely available process to guide States in considering whether to threaten or undertake preventive actions (or other uses of force). The Task Force believes that the potential benefits of formally acknowledging the possible use of legitimacy as a guide to conduct, specifying the standards and procedures it reflects, and encouraging their proper application, outweigh any danger that States may thereby be encouraged to engage in actions that continue to be considered illegal. Current State practice disregarding legal rules results from the inadequacies of those rules in enabling States to deal effectively with the realities of current threats. Refusing to provide guidance based on legitimacy is unlikely to result in greater adherence to legal rules that are consistently disregarded because of their perceived inadequacies. In any event, providing guidance as to the legitimacy of actions is no license for disregarding legal rules, but rather a method for helping to ensure that States take into account the international community's probable reactions, whether or not the actions meet strictly applied legal requirements.

It makes sense, therefore, to encourage States to undertake a systematic appraisal of the merits of any threat or use of preventive force, based not only on legal standards but also on the criteria relevant to legitimacy. Encouraging such appraisals should enhance the prospect that States that resort to preventive force will do so in a manner consistent with Charter purposes and the promotion of international peace and security.

Notes

Chapter 1

1. Chapter VII of the Charter contemplates that the Council would consider the need for sanctions and the use of force to deal with threats to international peace and security, and then would be able to call on the forces provided by Member States in accordance with Articles 43–47, under the supervision of a Military Staff Committee. The special agreements through which such forces were to be provided have never come into existence.

2. The 2006NSS sums up the 2002NSS in this manner: "We are fighting a new enemy with global reach. The United States can no longer simply rely on deterrence to keep the terrorists at bay or defensive measures to thwart them at the last moment. The fight must be taken to the enemy, to keep them on the run." 2006NSS at 8, available at http://georgewbush-whitehouse.archives.gov/nsc/nss/2006/nss2006.pdf.

3. This concept echoes the call in 1984 by then Secretary of State George P. Shultz for going "beyond passive defense to consider means of active prevention, preemption, and retaliation. Our goal must be to prevent and deter future terrorist acts." Shultz, George P., *Turmoil and Triumph* 648 (Charles Scribner's Sons, New York 1993). The need to act preventively was also stressed by high officials in the Clinton administration after the bombing of U.S. embassies in Africa, laying "down the framework which the Bush administration would take to the next level in the aftermath of September 11." Maogoto, Jackson Nyamuya, *Battling Terrorism: Legal Perspectives on the Use of Force and the War on Terror* (Ashgate Press, Burlington, Vt., 2005), p. 115 (Maogoto).

4. This report has been prepared by Abraham D. Sofaer, based on research and discussions of the Task Force, and on comments made by participants at the meetings with national security professionals and scholars. The report is not intended to reflect any particular position on any of the issues discussed, and except where specifically stated should not be understood to represent the views of the members of the Task Force who in addition to Chairmen Shultz and Blacker include:

Marc Abramowitz, Michael H. Armacost, Paul Brest, Gerhard Casper, Sidney Drell, David J. Holloway, Stephen D. Krasner, Henry S. Rowen, Scott D. Sagan, Kori Schake, and Abraham D. Sofaer. The Task Force has been assisted at various points by Matt Weingart, Catharine Kristian, Scott Tait, James E. Fanell, Scott F. Smith, Matthew Gunn, Megan Reiss, and Dennis Mandudzo. The Task Force has also had the invaluable assistance of Grace Goldberger throughout its work.

5. This Report was requested by UN Secretary General Kofi Annan to provide a "broad framework for collective security for the new century," and was issued by the United Nations in December 2004. It is available at www.un.org/secureworld/.

6. In his speech at the Task Force's Gotemba Conference, Secretary Shultz recognized that "circumstances will arise when difficult decisions about the use of preventive force must be confronted," but insisted that "every effort must be made to prevent the need for the use of preventive force." "An Ounce of Prevention is Worth a Pound of Cure," Paper delivered at the Conference on Preventive Force, Gotemba, Japan, May 25, 2008.

7. 2002NSS at Part V. "Full Text: Bush's National Security Strategy," *New York Times*, November 20, 2002, at: www.nytimes.com/2002/09/20/politics/20STEXT_FULL.html. The 2006NSS provides a more nuanced analysis, described below, but reaffirms (pp. 23, 37) that "we do not rule out the use of force before attacks occur, even if uncertainty remains as to the time and place of the enemy's attack" and that "we must be prepared to act alone if necessary."

8. Participants in the Stanford conference were: Marc Abramowitz, Michael H. Armacost, Arnold Beichman, Peter Berkowitz, Coit D. Blacker, Paul Brest, Gerhard Casper, Christopher F. Chyba, Jock Covey, Chester A. Crocker, Ivo H. Daalder, Larry Diamond, Sidney Drell, Stephen J. Flanagan, Victor Davis Hanson, John L. Hennessy, Thomas H. Henriksen, David Holloway, G. John Ikenberry, Paul Kern, Tod Lindberg, Thomas G. McInerney, John Mearsheimer, Steven E. Miller, Norman Naimark, Michael Radu, John Raisian, Peter Robinson, Henry Rowen, Scott D. Sagan, Kori Schake, George P. Shultz, Smita Singh, Anne-Marie Slaughter, Abraham D. Sofaer, Stephen J. Stedman, James B. Steinberg, David Victor, Allen S. Weiner, Marc Weller, and Daniel L. Zajac. The meeting had the benefit of a visit on May 27 from Secretary of State Condoleezza Rice, who commented on the issues.

9. Participants in the conference at Princeton were: Marc Abramowitz,

Gary Bass, Coit D. Blacker, Todd F. Buchwald, M. Elaine Bunn, William Burke-White, Joshua Busby, Thomas J. Christensen, Christopher F. Chyba, Elizabeth L. Colagiuri, Chester A. Crocker, Ivo H. Daalder, Mark T. Esper, James E. Fanell, Stephen J. Flanagan, Aaron L. Friedberg, Fatema Gunja, Edmund J. Hull, Robert L. Hutchings, G. John Ikenbery, Gregory Johnson, Robert O. Keohane, Henry A. Kissinger, Daniel Kurtzer, John McLaughlin, Michael Meese, Steven E. Miller, Andrew Moravcsik, William L. Nash, Barry S. Pavel, Victor E. Renuart, Jr., Henry Rowen, Kori Schake, George P. Shultz, Anne-Marie Slaughter, Scott F. Smith, Abraham D. Sofaer, James B. Steinberg, Jordan Tama, Gregory Treverton, Matthew Waxman, Ruth Wedgwood, Marc Weller, and Thomas Wright.

10. Participants in the conference at Bellagio were: Morten Aasland, Marc Abramowitz, William Burke-White, Gerhard Casper, Roberto D'Alimonte, Baldwin De Vidts, Sidney Drell, Espen Barth Eide, Ahmed Fathalla, David Hannay, David Holloway, Irina Isakova, Josef Joffe, Mordechai Kremnitzer, Steven E. Miller, Adam Roberts, Scott Sagan, Kori Schake, George P. Shultz, Radoslaw Sikorski, Abraham D. Sofaer, James Steinberg, Dimitry Suslov, Christian Tomuschat, Danilo Turk, and Pascal Vennesson.

11. Participants in the conference at Gotemba were: Muthiah Alagappa, Michael Armacost, Kim Beazley, Coit D. Blacker, William Burke-White, Sidney Drell, Han Sung-Joo, Syed Rifaat Hussain, Takashi Inoguchi, Jehangir Karamat, Stephen Krasner, Lee Hong-Koo, Martine Letts, Steven E. Miller, C. Raja Mohan, Ton Nu Thi Ninh, Leela K. Ponappa, Henry Rowen, George P. Shultz, Susan Sim, Anne-Marie Slaughter, Abraham D. Sofaer, Hitoshi Tanaka, Koji Watanabe, Wu Jianmin, Xiaobing Xu, and Huang Zhixiong.

12. Interviews were held with the following individuals: Antonio de Aguiar Patriota, Brazilian Ambassador to the U.S.; Arturo Sarukhan, Mexican Ambassador to the U.S.; Briggs Bomba, Africa Action; Elias Magembe, Producer, Voice of America; in addition to correspondence and calls with some African diplomats. The draft report was also presented to the Hoover Institution Task Force on National Security and Law in a meeting in Washington, D.C., on September 16, 2008, and benefited from the comments of the Members present: Kenneth Anderson, Peter Berkowitz, David Brady, Philip Bobbitt, Jack Goldsmith, Jessica Stern, Matthew Waxman, and Benjamin Wittes.

Chapter 2

1. See generally the excellent study, Mueller, Karl P., Castillo, Jasen J., Morgan, Forrest E., Pegahi, Negeen & Rosen, Brian, *Striking First: Preemptive and Preventive Attack in U.S. National Security Policy* (Rand 2006).
2. Letter of April 24, 1841, from Secretary of State Daniel Webster to Foreign Minister Henry Fox, in Stevens, Kenneth R., *Border Diplomacy* (Univ. of Alabama Press, Tuscaloosa, 1989), p. 105.
3. Charter of the United Nations, Art. 51.

Chapter 3

1. "A Secure Europe in a Better World," Brussels, December 12, 2003 ("EU Strategy") available at: http://ue.eu.int/uedocs/cmsUpload/78367.pdf.
2. The "gravest danger to freedom lies at the crossroads of radicalism and technology." Speech of President George W. Bush at 2002 Graduation Exercise of the U.S. Military Academy, West Point, N.Y.
3. The Alliance's Strategic Concept: A pproved in the Meeting of the North Atlantic Council in Washington, D.C., on April 23 and 24, 1999, available at: http://inesap.org/bulletin17/bul16art03.htm. The Istanbul Declaration, June 28, 2004, notes that the threats faced by NATO "have changed substantially" and include terrorism and proliferation of WMD. At: www.nato.int/docu/pr/2004/p04-097e.htm.
4. For example, Bruno Simma observed that the "German agreement with the legal position taken by the Alliance in the specific instance of Kosovo was not to be regarded as a 'green light' for similar NATO interventions in general. To quote Foreign Minister Kinkel before the Bundestag: 'The decision of NATO [on air strikes against the FRY] must not become a precedent. As far as the Security Council monopoly on force [Gewaltmonopol] is concerned, we must avoid getting on a slippery slope.'" Simma, Bruno, "NATO, The UN and the Use of Force: Legal Aspects," *EJIL* 1999 10(1). For a general overview of country support for the Kosovo intervention with the rationalization (legal or otherwise) for intervention, see Johnstone, Ian, "Security Council Deliberations: The Power of Better Argument," *EJIL* 2003 14(437).
5. Treaty of Amity and Cooperation in Southeast Asia. Chap. IV, Art. 13: "The High Contracting Parties shall have the determination and good

faith to prevent disputes from arising. In case disputes on matters directly affecting them should arise, especially disputes likely to disturb regional peace and harmony, they shall refrain from the threat or use of force and shall at all times settle such disputes among themselves through friendly negotiations." Available at: www.aseansec.org/1217 .htm.

6. See "UN Welcomes ASEAN Peacekeeping Force, Promises Help," *Jakarta Post*, February 27, 2004.

7. "Interview: John Howard." *Ninemsn, Australia*. December 1, 2002, at: http://sunday.ninemsn.com.au/sunday/political_transcripts/article_1192.asp.

8. "Mahathir attacks Howard's pre-emptive strike comments," December 3, 2002. From the radio show *PM*, on ABC local radio, Australia, at: www.abc.net.au/pm/stories/s740039.htm.

9. Bolton, David, "The Tyranny of Difference: Perceptions of Australian Defence Policy in Southeast Asia," Working Paper No. 384 (National Library of Australia, Canberra, 2003).

10. "Interview of External Affairs Minister Shri. Yashwant Sinha with AFP," April 2, 2003, at: http://mea.gov.in/interview/2003/04/02i01.htm.

11. See Chap. IV, Art. 19 in the Charter of the Organization of American States at: www.oas.org/juridico/English/charter.html. See also the Inter-American Convention against Terrorism at: www.oas.org/xxxiiga/english/docs_en/docs_items/AGres1840_02.htm.

12. See ECOWAS: Protocol Relating to the Mechanism for Conflict Prevention, Management, Resolution, Peace-Keeping and Security (Art. 25) at: http://www.comm.ecowas.int/sec/index.php?id=ap101299&lang=en; SADC: Protocol on Politics, Defence and Security Co-Operation (Art. 11) at www.sadc.int/. See AU: African Charter on Democracy, Elections, and Governance (Art. 23) at: www.africa-union.org/root/au/Documents/Treaties/text/Charter%20on%20Democracy.pdf. These developments are described in Jeremy I. Levitt, "Pro-Democratic Intervention in Africa," 24 *Wis. Int'l. L.J.* 785 (2006) (Levitt).

13. The Conflict Protocol (Art. 25) provides that ECOWAS may take action in internal conflicts that threaten to trigger a humanitarian disaster, pose a serious threat to regional stability, have caused a serious and massive violation of human rights and the rule of law, or where an effort has been made to overthrow a democratically elected government.

14. See Protocol A/SP1/01, Democracy and Good Governance Supplementary to the Protocol relating to the Mechanism for Conflict Prevention, Management, Resolutions, Peacekeeping, and Security, Sect. VII, available at: www.comm.ecowas.int/sec/index.php?id=protocole&lang=en.

15. Levitt, p. 21.

16. Decisions of the Assembly are made by consensus, or failing which by a two-thirds majority of Member States eligible to vote. Art. 7, Constitutive Act; Rule 18, Rules of Procedure of the Assembly, available at: www.africa-union.org/root/au/AboutAu/Constitutive_Act_en.htm.

17. See generally Kioko, Ben, "The right of intervention under the African Union's Constitutive Act: From non-interference to non-intervention," IRRC December 2003, Vol. 85, pp. 807–824, at 824. He describes the African Union as having "moved away from non-interference or non-intervention—which is a cardinal principle in both the United Nations Charter and the Constitutive Act of the African Union—to what could be referred to as the doctrine of 'non-indifference.'" Id. 819.

18. Konaré, Alpha Oumar, "Preventing and Combating Terrorism in Africa." At: www.africa-union.org/Terrorism/terrorism2.htm.

19. Deng, Francis M., Kimaro, Sadikiel, Lyons, Terrence, Rothchild, Donald, & Zartman, I. William, *Sovereignty as Responsibility: Conflict Management in Africa* (Brookings Institution Press, Washington, D.C., 1996), pp. 32–33.

Chapter 4

1. See "Joint Doctrine for Military Operations Other Than War (MOOTW)," *Joint Pub 3-07* (June 16, 1995).

2. Useful studies of national law enforcement methods for preventing terrorist acts, both before and after September 11, 2001, include: Beckman, James, *Comparative Legal Approaches to Homeland Security and Anti-Terrorism* (Ashgate Press, Burlington, Vt., 2007); Ramraj, Victor V., Hor, Michael, & Roach, Kent, eds., *Global Anti-Terrorism Law and Policy* (Cambridge Univ. Press, New York, 2005); Jacobson, Michael, *The West at War: U.S. and European Counterterrorism Efforts, Post September 11* (Washington Institute for Near East Policy, Washington, D.C., 2006).

3. Oliver "Buck" Revell, "The Role of Law Enforcement Agencies in Combating Terrorism," in Yonah Alexander, ed., *Terrorists in Our Midst* (Praeger Publishers, Westport, Conn., 2009).

4. Former Attorney General of the U.S. John Ashcroft conceded that the pre-2001 system of law enforcement over which he presided was "a tragedy waiting to happen, a system destined to fail." *Never Again: Securing America and Restoring Justice* 144 (Center Street Press, New York, 2006).

5. National Strategy for Homeland Security, July 2002. Available at: www .whitehouse.gov/homeland/book/.

6. Proposal for a Council Framework Decision on the use of Passenger Name Record (PNR) for Law Enforcement Purposes {SEC (2007) 1422} {SEC(2007) 1453} was sent to the EU in late 2007. PNR analysis has already been adopted in the U.S. and Canada, and has a pilot program in effect in the U.K. with the hopes of tracking suspicious activity and using that knowledge to prevent terrorist attacks through law enforcement. At www.europarl.europa.eu/oeil/FindByProcnum.do? lang=2&procnum=CNS/2007/0237.

7. For example, an attack by the terrorist organization Jemaah Islamiyah to blow up American, British, Israeli, and Australian embassies in Singapore was prevented in December 2001. On June 2, 2007, four suspected terrorists were arrested with plans to blow up John F. Kennedy Airport in New York through the pipeline that runs under Queens. For full details of this plot, see NEFA Report No. 16 "Target America," available at: www.nefafoundation.org/miscellaneous/FeaturedDocs/ nefajfkplot1008.pdf.

8. The State Department notes the following successes in anti-terrorism work, including "close cooperation between Pakistani, British and United States law enforcement agencies which exposed the August London Heathrow bomb plot . . . . [I]n 2006 the Canadians disrupted a major extremist plot on their own territory and arrested 18 individuals in Toronto and . . . in March the Australians arrested three suspected terrorists in Melbourne as part of an ongoing counterterrorism operation which disrupted a significant threat to that community." Country Reports on Terrorism 2007 (2008) p. 10, 29, 30, 140, and 151–152, available at: www.state.gov/documents/ organization/105904.pdf.

9. See H.R. 3199, USA PATRIOT Improvement and Reauthorization Act of 2005, at www.govtrack.us/congress/billtext.xpd?bill=h109-3199.

10. The Australian Anti-Terrorism Act (No. 2) 2005 allows the Attorney General and later the courts to issue interim and confirmed court orders to hold a suspect for up to a year without being charged. www.comlaw.gov.au/ComLaw/Legislation/Act1.nsf/asmade/bytitle/9249 AE71DF443FDFCA2570D80024D5A0?OpenDocument. Chapter II in the Singaporean Internal Security Act allows the preventive detention of individuals for up to two years. At: http://statutes.agc.gov.sg/non_version/cgi-bin/cgi_retrieve.pl?actno=REVED-143.

11. Detention pending deportation is used in many States to prevent individuals considered dangerous from engaging in illegal conduct or fleeing to a safe haven. The U.K., for example, detained the radical cleric Abu Qatada, while seeking his deportation. He is believed to have counseled Richard Reid and Zacarias Moussaoui, among others, and tapes of his sermons are reported to have been found in the Hamburg apartment used by the plotters of the September 11, 2001, attacks in the U.S. "Britain Orders Radical Islamic Cleric Back to Jail," *New York Times*, December 3, 2008, p. A6, col. 3.

12. U.S. laws that provide such authority include the Comprehensive Crime Control Act of 1984, 18 U.S.C. 1203 (requiring permission of foreign government), and the Omnibus Diplomatic Security and Anti-Terrorism Act of 1986, 18 U.S.C. 2331 (authority to prosecute persons who assault U.S. nationals abroad or conspire to do so).

13. INTERPOL initially did little to facilitate cooperation on terrorism-related issues, but has increased its role since the 1980s. The European Union has a Terrorism Coordinator with authority and responsibility that applies within all the EU States. See Declaration on Combating Terrorism, March 25, 2004, at: www.consilium.europa.eu/ueDocs/cms_Data/docs/pressData/en/ec/79637.pdf. A valuable summary of international cooperation on terrorism in Asia was presented at the Task Force meeting in Japan by Kim Beazley, former Australian Minister of Defense and currently Professorial Fellow at the University of Western Australia. The presentation was compiled by Lucy Roberts, Senior Research Officer at the University, and can be obtained at Lucy.Roberts@uwa.edu.au.

14. In November 2002, the CIA used a Predator drone within Yemen to target Al Qaeda operative Abu Ali al-Harithi. See "Q & A: Targeted Killings," *New York Times*, January 25, 2006, at: www.nytimes.com/cfr/international/slot3_012506.html?scp=1&sq=Abu%20Ali%20al-Harithi&st=cse.

15. See Laflin, Melanie M., "Kidnapped Terrorists: Bringing International Criminals to Justice through Irregular Rendition and Other Quasi-legal Options," 26 *J. Legis*. 315 (2000). Formal extradition in the United States is governed by 18 U.S.C. § 3184 and 18 U.S.C. § 3181.

16. Human rights organizations fault the secret "extraordinary renditions" as a method for circumventing conventions outlawing torture by flying suspects to countries with lax practices and then interrogating them with extraordinary means. Amnesty International found that European countries have not taken steps to prevent further renditions. *State of Denial: Europe's Role in Rendition and Secret Detention*, Amnesty International, June 2008, at: www.amnestyusa.org/stoptorture/pdf/Europe%20renditions%20whole%20doc%20low%20res.pdf. The U.S. Court of Appeals for the Second Circuit agreed to rehear the case of Canadian Maher Arar, who was sent to Syria to be interrogated. The case was originally dismissed on the basis that hearing the arguments could reveal national security information, but proceedings recommenced on December 9, 2008. "Appeals Court Hears Case of Canadian Citizen Sent by U.S. to Syria," *New York Times*, December 9, 2008, at: www.nytimes.com/2008/12/10/nyregion/10arar.html?fta=y. The Obama administration, as in past administrations, supports the state secrets privilege within the extraordinary rendition process, arguing that extraordinary rendition lawsuits against the government and contracted parties "would pose an unacceptable risk to national security." "Feds want secrecy over alleged torture flights," *San Francisco Chronicle*, June 13, 2009, at: www.sfgate.com/cgi-bin/article.cgi?f=/c/a/2009/06/13/BAD5186LUA.DTL. The Council of Europe investigated rendition by the CIA in a report written by Swiss *rapporteur* Dick Marty. Mr. Marty found that rendition programs are in place in the European countries of Russia, Poland, Romania, Germany, Macedonia, and Italy and that "the scope of the executive's reserved area, exempted by virtue of state secrecy and national security from parliamentary and judicial review under legislation or in accordance with

practice dating from the worst period of the Cold War, must be reconsidered to take into account the principles of democracy and rule of law." "Alleged secret detentions in Council of Europe member states," Committee on Legal Affairs and Human Rights, January 22, 2006, available at: http://assembly.coe.int/Main.asp?link=/CommitteeDocs/2006/20060124_Jdoc032006_E.htm.

17. The United Nations Convention of the Law of the Seas states that "the criminal jurisdiction of the coastal State should not be exercised on board a foreign ship passing through the territorial sea . . . save only in the following cases: if such measures are necessary for the suppression of illicit traffic in narcotic drugs or psychotropic substances." (Part II, Art. 27.1(d)). Full text available at: www.un.org/Depts/los/convention_agreements/texts/unclos/closindx.htm.

18. Under the Proliferation Security Initiative (PSI), British and American intelligence services watched as centrifuge parts, manufactured in Malaysia, were sent to Dubai. From there, they were loaded onto the German vessel, the BBC *China*, bound for Libya in late summer 2003. The vessel was seized by Italian and German authorities (with the permission of the ship's owner) and taken to an Italian port, where they discovered the centrifuge parts, falsely labeled "used machinery parts." The Libyan government soon thereafter abandoned its pursuit of nuclear weapons. At: http://fpc.state.gov/documents/organization/48624.pdf.

19. *United States v. Yunis*, 681 F. Supp. 896 (D.D.C. 1988).

20. Id 16. U.N. Convention on the Law of the Seas (December 10, 1982), Part VII, Art. 100-107, available at www.un.org/Depts/los/convention_agreements/texts/unclos/closindx.htm.

21. See the Convention for the Suppression of Unlawful Acts against the Safety of Maritime Navigation (1988), available at: http://untreaty.un.org/English/Terrorism/Conv8.pdf.

22. The PSI started as a response to Spain finding 15 SCUD missiles hidden among 40,000 bags of cement leaving North Korea on a freighter. Spain considered itself unable to confiscate the weapons under international law. The PSI is described as "a global effort that aims to stop trafficking of weapons of mass destruction (WMD), their delivery systems, and related materials to and from states and non-state actors of proliferation concern . . . [and] relies on voluntary actions by states

that are consistent with national legal authorities." Overview available at: www.state.gov/t/isn/c10390.htm.

23. The United Nation's Universal Declaration of Human Rights, passed December 10, 1948, states in Article 30: "Nothing in this Declaration may be interpreted as implying for any State, group, or person any right to engage in any activity or to perform any act aimed at the destruction of any of the rights and freedoms set forth herein."

24. A comparative study of the British and French responses to the Islamic terrorist threat explains the tendency of agencies to revert to prior practices, resulting in enhanced prevention but increased difficulty in the U.K. in obtaining admissible evidence for prosecutions. Foley, Frank, "Reforming Counterterrorism: Institutions and Organizational Routines in France and the UK," forthcoming in *Security Studies* (2009).

25. See the 2006 report "Mobilizing Information to Prevent Terrorism: Accelerating Development of a Trusted Information Sharing Environment," conducted by the Markle Foundation Task Force. Report available at: www.markle.org/markle_programs/policy_for_a_networked_society/national_security/projects/taskforce_national_security.php#report1.

26. Franck, Thomas M., "On Proportionality of Countermeasures in International Law," 102 *A.J.I.L.* 715 (2008).

27. Doyle, Michael W., *Striking First: Preemption and Prevention in International Conflict* (Princeton University Press, Princeton, N.J., 2008) pp. 85–88.

28. S/RES/1368 (12 September 2001), S/RES/1373 (September 28, 2001). Prediction methodology is beyond the scope of this report. Officials considering such issues should utilize the full range of available methodologies in attempting to predict future conduct as a basis for using preventive force. See, e.g., Bueno de Mesquita, Bruce, *Predicting Politics* (Ohio State Univ. Press, Columbus, Ohio, 2001).

29. Transcript of Osama bin Laden's October interview, February 5, 2002. "Those men who sacrificed themselves in New York and Washington, they are the spokesmen of the nation's conscience. They are the nation's conscience that saw they have to avenge against the oppression. . . . Not all terrorism is cursed; some terrorism is blessed . . . America won't get out of this crisis until it gets out of the Arabian Peninsula, and until it

stops its support of Israel.... In this fighting between Islam and the crusaders, we will continue our jihad." At: http://archives.cnn.com/2002/WORLD/asiapcf/south/02/05/binladen.transcript/index.html.

30. S.J.Res. 23 Sec. 2a: "That the President is authorized to use all necessary and appropriate force against those nations, organizations, or persons he determines planned, authorized, committed, or aided the terrorist attacks that occurred on September 11, 2001, or harbored such organizations or persons."

31. The Bush administration reportedly authorized the use of force by Executive Order against the Al Qaeda network anywhere in the world. Actions were actually approved, however, only in a limited number of States, including Pakistan, Somalia, and Syria, among the fifteen to twenty States believed to have Al Qaeda members. "Secret Order Lets U.S. Raid Al Qaeda in Many Countries," *New York Times*, November 10, 2008, p. A1, col. 1.

32. Greenwood, Christopher, "War, Terrorism, and International Law," 56 *Current L. Probs.* 525 (2004). ("A war on terrorism, if such a concept can have any legal meaning, cannot have a greater effect than a war between States. In particular, neither type of war could provide a legal justification for military action against a State which was accused of harbouring Al-Qaeda.")

33. *The Public Committee Against Torture in Israel v. The Government of Israel* (2006) HCJ 769/02. See the Protocol Additional to the Geneva Conventions of August 12, 1949, and relating to the Protection of Victims of Non-International Armed Conflicts (Protocol II, June 8, 1977), available at: http://www.icrc.org/ihl.nsf/FULL/475?OpenDocument. The Court ruled, however, that a terrorist may regain noncombatant status by refraining from participating in attacks for a sufficiently long period, the precise length of which the Court did not specify.

34. According to The Hague Convention V, The Laws of War: Rights and Duties of Neutral Powers and Persons in Case of War on Land (October 18, 1907), Chapter 1: "Belligerents are forbidden to move troops or convoys of either munitions of war or supplies across the territory of a neutral Power" (Art. 2); "Corps of combatants cannot be formed nor recruiting agencies opened on the territory of a neutral Power to assist the belligerents" (Art. 4); and "A neutral Power must not allow any of the acts referred to in Articles 2 to 4 to occur on its territory. It

is not called upon to punish acts in violation of its neutrality *unless the said acts have been committed on its own territory.*" (Art. 5) (Emphasis added.) According to the convention, a State is required to prevent belligerents from entering its territory, or to allow a State to enter its territory to retrieve the belligerents. Hague Convention V, available at: http://avalon.law.yale.edu/20th_century/hague05.asp.

35. The 1958 Convention of the High Seas, Art. 23, and the 1982 Convention on the Law of Sea, Art. 11, outline the right of "hot pursuit." Convention available at: http://untreaty.un.org/ilc/texts/instruments/english/conventions/8_1_1958_high_seas.pdf. The right is effective until the belligerent ship enters its own waters or the waters of a third State. After entering the waters of a third State, the Laws of War, Duties for Neutrality require the neutral State to respond; the neutral State may allow the first State to continue its pursuit, or conduct the pursuit itself. The first State may also claim self-defense in order to continue the pursuit.

36. In 2008, the *New York Times* reported on a leaked document from 2005 that claimed that "American military forces in Iraq were authorized to pursue former members of Saddam Hussein's government and terrorists across Iraq's borders into Iran and Syria." See "Leak on Cross-Border Chases from Iraq," *New York Times*, February 4, 2008, at: www.nytimes.com/2008/02/04/washington/04rules.html.

37. Gray, Christine, *The Use of Force in International Law* (Oxford Univ. Press, New York, 2000), pp. 102–104 (Gray).

38. Many uses of force without Security Council approval have taken place to expel colonial powers, and most have been accepted by the international community. Prominent examples include Indonesia's actions in Western New Guinea in 1960–62, eventually causing the Dutch to withdraw, India's action driving Portugal from Goa in 1961, and the many anti-colonial uses of force in Africa and Asia. States often use force against each other in asserting border claims, sometimes causing significant casualties as in the case of the disputes between India and China, and between several Latin American States. Many of these disputes are described in Weisbird, A. Mark, *Use of Force: The Practice of States Since World War II* (Penn State Univ. Press, University Park, Penn., 1997) (Weisbird).

39. This chapter relies on sources that collect and discuss post-Charter interventions in considerable detail, especially Weisbird; Franck,

Thomas M., *Recourse to Force: State Action Against Threats and Armed Attacks* (Cambridge Univ. Press 2002) (Franck); Murphy, Sean A., *Humanitarian Intervention* (Cambridge Univ. Press, Cambridge, UK, 1996) (Murphy).

40. Professor Derek Bowett states: "Action undertaken for the purpose of, and limited to, the defence of a State's political independence, territorial integrity, the lives and property of its nationals (and even to protect its economic independence) cannot by definition involve a threat or use of force 'against the territorial integrity or political independence' of any other state." Bowett, Derek, quoted in Maogoto, p. 167.

41. "The Suez Crisis: An Affair to Remember." *The Economist.* July 27, 2006.

42. Gray, p. 64.

43. Franck, pp. 79–81; 117–21.

44. Yates, Lawrence A., "Power Pack: US Intervention in the Dominican Republic, 1965–1966" *Leavenworth Papers No. 15, Combat Studies Institute.* At: www-cgsc.army.mil/carl/resources/csi/yates/yates.asp#3-2.

45. Shultz, George P., *Turmoil and Triumph: My Years as Secretary of State* (Scribner Press, New York, 1993), pp. 323–345.

46. Cole, Ronald H., "Operation Urgent Fury: Grenada," *Joint History Office, Office of the Joint Chiefs of Staff* (Washington, D.C., 1997), at: www.dtic.mil/doctrine/jel/history/urgfury.pdf.

47. Henriksen, Thomas H., *American Power After the Berlin Wall* (Palgrave Macmillan, New York, 2007), pp. 28–29.

48. In his address on December 21, 1989, following the U.S. invasion of Panama to oust Noriega, President George H.W. Bush stated that "the goals of the United States have been to safeguard the lives of Americans, to defend democracy in Panama, to combat drug trafficking and to protect the integrity of the Panama Canal Treaty." The Panama Canal Treaties of 1977, also known as the Torrijos-Carter Treaties, provided for full control of the Panama Canal to be transferred from the United States to Panama, which occurred on December 31, 1999. See the transcript of President Bush's speech at: http://query.nytimes.com/gst/fullpage.html?res=950DE4D8143FF932A15751C1A96F948260&sec=&spon=&pagewanted=all. See article related to the handover of the Panama Canal at: http://query.nytimes.com/gst/fullpage.html?res=9A0DEFDB1238F932A05751C1A96F958260&&scp=1&sq=panama%20canal%20december%2031,%201999&st=cse.

49. E.g., Gray, p. 65; Henkin, Louis et al., *Right V. Might: International Law and the Use of Force*, 2nd ed. (Council on Foreign Relations Press, New York, 1991).

50. "Terror Convulses Rwandan Capital as Tribes Battle," *New York Times*, April 9, 1994, at: www.nytimes.com/1994/04/09/world/terror-convulses-rwandan-capital-as-tribes.

51. Wesiburd, pp. 277–278.

52. See "Capture of Hijackers; Action against Terrorists: 4 Incidents in Decade," *New York Times*, October 11, 1985. Available for purchase at: www.nytimes.com/1985/10/11/world/capture-of-hijackers-action-against-terrorists-4-incidents-in-decade.html?scp=2&sq=%E2%80%9CCapture%20of%20Hijackers;%20Action%20against%20Terrorists:%204%20Incidents%20in%20Decade%E2%80%9D%20&st=cse.

53. Weisburd, pp. 37–40.

54. Hijacking of airplanes is illegal under various treaties, such as The Hague Convention for the Suppression of the Unlawful Seizure of Aircraft, which entered into force October 14, 1971. "Hostages Freed as Israelis Raid Uganda Airport; Commandos in 3 Planes Rescue 105-Casualties Unknown/ Israelis Raid Uganda Airport And Free Hijackers' Hostages," *New York Times*, July 4, 1976. Available for purchase at: http://select.nytimes.com/gst/abstract.html?res=F60816FA38591B728DDDAD0894DF405B868BF1D3&scp=1&sq=%E2%80%9CHostages%20Freed%20as%20Israelis%20Raid%20Uganda%20Airport;%20Commandos%20in%203%20Planes%20Rescue%20105-Casualties%20Unknown%20Israelis%20Raid%20Uganda%20Airport%20And%20Free%20Hijackers%27%20Hostages%E2%80%9D%20&st=cse.

55. UN Secretary-General Kurt Waldheim condemned Israel's actions, saying: "I have not got all the details, but it seems to be clear that Israeli aircraft have landed in Entebbe and this constitutes a serious violation of the sovereignty of a State Member [Uganda] of the United Nations." Excerpts from United Nations Security Council Debate on the Entebbe Incident, 13 *UN Monthly Chronicle* (August-September 1976).

56. Ugandan president Idi Amin asked the Security Council to condemn Israel for infringing Ugandan sovereignty with the raid on July 9, 1976. The Council refused. The following statements were made by various countries in regard to their decision not to condemn Israel:

"Sweden, although unable to reconcile the Israeli action with the strict rules of the Charter, did not find it possible to join in a condemnation in such a case. . . . The Air France hijacking was terminated in an extraordinary circumstance—military action by a State within the territory of another State. Although the motives as well as the circumstances which led Israel to take such action were presented in detail, nevertheless there was an act of violation by Israel of the sovereignty of Uganda." Japan reserved its opinion as to whether the Israeli military action had or had not met the conditions required for the exercise of the right of self-defence recognized under international law, as the Israeli representative contended ". . . Israel's action in rescuing the hostages necessarily involved a temporary breach of the territorial integrity of Uganda. Normally, such a breach would be impermissible under the Charter. However, there was a well established right to use limited force for the protection of one's own nationals from an imminent threat of injury or death in a situation where the State in whose territory they were located was either unwilling or unable to protect them. The right, flowing from the right of self-defence, was limited to such use of force as was necessary and appropriate to protect threatened nationals from injury." Excerpts from United Nations Security Council Debate on the Entebbe Incident, 13 *UN Monthly Chronicle* (August-September 1976).

57. "U.S. Attempt to Rescue Hostages in Teheran Fails; Equipment Trouble Blamed for Aborted Mission; 8 Die in Air Mishap in Iran's Desert," *Facts on File World News Digest*, April 25, 1980.

58. Weisburd, pp. 285–86.

59. Franck, pp. 88–89. Italy refused to allow the U.S. to take the terrorists for prosecution, and allowed Abbas and other leaders to escape. Several of the hijackers were tried and sentenced to prison terms, however, and Abbas was tried in absentia and given a life sentence as the mastermind behind the crime. Maogoto, p. 99.

60. "Sticky legal battles await for captured Somali pirates," *Christian Science Monitor*, April 14, 2009, at: www.csmonitor.com/2009/0415/p06s07-wogn.html.

61. "French raid pirate ship, US seeks to freeze assets," April 15, 2009. At: http://news.yahoo.com/s/ap/20090415/ap_on_re_af/piracy. See also:

"Dutch free Yemeni captives from pirates," *New York Times*, April 18, 2009, at: www.nytimes.com/2009/04/19/world/africa/19pirates.html?_r=1&ref=global-home.

62. See Security Council Resolutions 1814 (2008), 1816 (2008), and 1838 (2008).

63. Israeli Corporal Gilad Shalit was captured in a cross-border raid by Hamas and other militant groups in 2006. In February 2009, Hamas was "demanding the release of as many as 1,400 Palestinian security prisoners in Israeli jails in return for the captive soldier." See "Israel Puts Cpl. Shalit's Release on Table in Gaza Talks," *New York Times*, February 19, 2009, at: www.nytimes.com/2009/02/19/world/middleeast/19mideast.html?scp=1&sq=Shalit%20Israel%20raid%20demand%20release&st=cse. A similar deal was brokered in 2004. Israel agreed to release 400 Hezbollah prisoners in exchange for an Israeli businessman and the remains of three soldiers. "Israel Agrees to Free Arabs in a Swap with Militants," *New York Times*, January 25, 2004, at: www.nytimes.com/2004/01/25/world/israel-agrees-to-free-arabs-in-a-swap-with-militants.html?scp=17&sq=israel%20captives%20palestinian%20exchange&st=cse.

64. The seizure could have been justified on the grounds that the Sheikh was responsible for many attacks on Israel and the killing of Israeli civilians. "Just After Deadline, Israel Offered to Trade Prisoners," *New York Times*, August 1, 1981, at: www.nytimes.com/1989/08/01/world/just-after-deadline-israel-offered-to-trade-prisoners.html?scp=4&sq=Sheikh%20Abdel%20Karim%20Obeid%20&st=cse&pagewanted=1.

65. "Jurisdiction Over a Person Abducted from a Foreign Country: Alvarez Machain Case Revisited," *Journal of Malaysian and Comparative Law* (4) 2004, at: www.commonlii.org/my/journals/JMCL/2004/4.html.

66. Lowenfield, Andreas F. "Male Captus, Bene Detentus: U.S. Law Enforcement Abroad: The Constitution and International Law," 84 *A.J.I.L.* 444 (1990). The doctrine was originally questioned but upheld in an extradition case, *Ker v. Illinois*, 119 U.S. 436 (1886).

67. Security Council Resolution 138 (June 23, 1960). At: www.un.org/documents/sc/res/1960/scres60.htm.

68. *United States v. Alvarez-Machain*, 504 U.S. 655 (1992).

69. Weisburd, pp. 271–72, 292–93. See also Security Council S/17796/Rev. 1, February 6, 1986. Vetoed: 10–1 (US), with 4 abstentions (Australia, Denmark, France, UK).

70. "1978: Egyptian forces die in Cyprus gunfight," *BBC On This Day*, February 19, 1978, at: http://news.bbc.co.uk/onthisday/hi/dates/stories/february/19/newsid_2565000/2565701.stm.

71. International conventions outlawing the hijacking of planes include the Convention on Offences and Certain Other Acts Committed on Board Aircraft (the Tokyo Convention) of 1963, the Convention for the Suppression of Unlawful Seizure of Aircraft (The Hague Convention) of 1970, and the Convention for the Suppression of Unlawful Acts Against the Safety of Civil Aviation (the Montreal Convention) of 1971. Hijacking of ships is outlawed in the Convention on the High Seas of 1958, and the Convention for the Suppression of the Unlawful Acts against the Safety of Maritime Navigation of 1988.

72. Vienna Convention on Consular Relations of 1963, Art. 40. Available at: http://untreaty.un.org/ilc/texts/instruments/english/conventions/9_2_1963.pdf. See also The Convention on the Prevention and Punishment of Crimes against Internationally Protected Persons, including Diplomatic Agents, December 14, 1973. Available at: http://untreaty.un.org/ilc/texts/instruments/english/conventions/9_4_1973.pdf.

73. The International Convention against the Taking of Hostages (December 17, 1979). Available at: http://untreaty.un.org/English/Terrorism/Conv5.pdf.

74. "U.S. Strike Hits Insurgent at Safehouse," *New York Times*, June 8, 2006, at: www.nytimes.com/2006/06/08/world/middleeast/08cnd-iraq.html?_r=1&scp=2&sq=al-Zarqawi&st=cse.

75. Chapter 4, *The 9/11 Commission Report: Final Report of the National Commission on Terrorist Attacks upon the United States* (July 22, 2004), at: http://govinfo.library.unt.edu/911/report/911Report.pdf.

76. "Israelis Kill Chief of Pro-Iran Shiites in South Lebanon," *New York Times*, February 17, 1992, at: www.nytimes.com/1992/02/17/world/israelis-kill-chief-of-pro-iran-shiites-in-south-lebanon.html?scp=2&sq=Sheikh%20Abbas%20Musawi&st=cse.

77. HCJ 769/02, *The Public Committee Against Torture in Israel v. The Government of Israel* C.31: "The basic approach is thus as follows: a civil-

ian—that is, a person who does not fall into the category of combatant—must refrain from directly participating in hostilities (*see* Dieter
Fleck, *The Handbook of Humanitarian Law in Armed Conflicts* (Oxford
University Press, 2008) at p. 210). A civilian who violates that law and
commits acts of combat does not lose his status as a civilian, but as long
as he is taking a direct part in hostilities he does not enjoy—during that
time—the protection granted to a civilian. He is subject to the risks of
attack like those to which a combatant is subject, without enjoying the
rights of a combatant, e.g., those granted to a prisoner of war. True, his
status is that of a civilian, and he does not lose that status while he is
directly participating in hostilities. However, he is a civilian performing the function of a combatant. As long as he performs that function,
he is subject to the risks which that function entails and ceases to enjoy
the protection granted to a civilian from attack (see Watkin, Kenneth,
"Controlling the Use of Force: A Role for Human Rights Norms in
Contemporary Armed Conflict," 98 *A.J.I.L.* 1 (2004)).

78. Executive Order 11,905, Sec. 5*(g)*, *Prohibition of Assassination*: "No
employee of the United States Government shall engage in, or conspire
to engage in, political assassination."

79. Colonel W. Hays Parks, "The Memorandum on Executive Order 12333
and Assassination" wrote that an *"assassination* involves murder of a
targeted individual for political purposes" (Annex A). The memorandum is archived at the Harvard Kennedy School at: http://www.hks
.harvard.edu/cchrp/Use%20of%20Force/October%202002/Parks_
final.pdf.

80. Col. Parks' position is consistent with a cleared speech by then Legal
Adviser Abraham D. Sofaer, "Terrorism, the Law, and the National Defense," 126 *Military L. Rev.* 89, 116–121 (1989).

81. On Nov. 23, 2006, former KGB agent Alexander V. Litvinenko (a Russian fugitive with British citizenship) was poisoned in London, apparently by former KGB bodyguard Andrei K. Lugovoi. Russia subsequently refused to extradite Lugovoi to be tried in the UK, claiming
that extradition is against the Russian Constitution. "Britain Regrets
Russia's Refusal To Extradite In Poison Case," *New York Times,* July 11,
2007, at: http://query.nytimes.com/gst/fullpage.html?res=9A0CE2DB
113EF932A25754C0A9619C8B63&scp=1&sq=united+kingdom+pois
on+russia&st=nyt.

82. In HCJ 769/02, *The Public Committee against Torture in Israel v. The Government of Israel*, the Court ruled that Israel is in a continuous situation of armed conflict with terrorist organizations active in Judea, Samaria, and the Gaza strip. Applying Article 51(3) of the 1977 Additional Protocol I to the Geneva Conventions, it ruled that civilians lose the protection of that treaty "for such time as they take a direct part in hostilities." Even such individuals, however, the Court ruled, are not to be harmed unless necessary to prevent future attacks, and operations aimed at them must make every effort to minimize harm to others. Such operations may be judicially reviewed retroactively, with deference to the military for reasonable judgments. The Court also suggested compensation for innocent victims.

83. Kaplan, Eben, "Q&A: Targeted Killings," Council on Foreign Relations, January 25, 2006. On the issue of how targeted killings are authorized: "Experts say a presidential 'finding,' a declaration that a covert operation is in the national interest, gives the authority to carry out covert operations such as targeted killings." On the issue of a review process before authorizing a targeted attack: "the type of review depends on what organization is carrying out the attack. If the U.S. military is involved, there is 'a very sophisticated target-review process that checks and cross-checks any potential target with regard to constraints of international law, appropriateness of choice of munitions, blast effects as they relate to collateral damage, etc.' says Scott Silliman, executive director of Duke University's Center on Law, Ethics, and National Security." At: www.nytimes.com/cfr/international/slot3_012506.html?_r=1&pagewanted=print&oref=slogin.

84. "In Israel, a Divisive Struggle Over Targeted Killings" *The Washington Post*, August 27, 2006. "More than half of all targeted operations have been called off, a senior military source said, because of danger to non-combatants. The current air force chief, Maj. Gen. Elyezer Shkedy, said in an interview that collateral damage had been decreasing from one civilian death per assassination in 2002 to one civilian death for every 25 terrorists killed in 2005."

85. "Jordan Expecting Israel to Release More Palestinians From Jail," *New York Times*, October 5, 1997, at: www.nytimes.com/1997/10/05/world/jordan-expecting-israel-to-release-more-palestinians-from-jail.html?scp=15&sq=khaled%20mashaal%20assassination%20attempt&st=cse.

86. S/Res/347 (24 April 1974).

87. "US Jets Hit 'Terrorist Centers' in Libya, Reagan Warns of New Attacks if Needed," *New York Times*, April 15, 1986. President Reagan stated in a speech about the Libya bombings: "We believe that this pre-emptive action against his terrorist installations will not only diminish Colonel Qaddafi's capacity to export terror, it will provide him with incentives and reasons to alter his criminal behavior." At: www.nytimes .com/1986/04/15/politics/15REAG.html.

88. UN GA, A/RES/41/38 (November 20, 1986): "Condemns the military attack perpetrated against the Socialist People's Libyan Arab Jamahiriya on 15 April 1986, which constitutes a violation of the Charter of the United Nations and of international law."

89. McWhinney, Edward, *Aerial Piracy and International Terrorism: The Illegal Diversion of Aircraft and International Law* (Kluwer Law International Press, 1987), p. 176.

90. "U.S. responds to attack by Iraqi government," Transcript, Address of President Clinton to the Nation, June 26, 1993: "Our intent was to target Iraq's capacity to support violence against the United States and other nations and to deter Saddam Hussein from supporting such outlaw behavior in the future. Therefore, we directed our action against the facility associated with Iraq's support of terrorism, while making every effort to minimize the loss of innocent life." Buhite, Russel D., eds., *Calls to Arms: Presidential Speeches, Messages, and Declarations of War*, (Scholarly Resources, Wilmington, Del., 2003), p. 322.

91. Excerpts from address by President Clinton (August 20, 1998): "Two weeks ago, 12 Americans and nearly 300 Kenyans and Tanzanians lost their lives. And another 5,000 were wounded when our embassies in Nairobi and Dar es Salaam were bombed. . . . Based on this information, we have high confidence that these bombings were planned, financed and carried out by the organization bin Laden leads. . . . The United States carried out simultaneous strikes against terrorist facilities and infrastructure in Afghanistan. Our forces targeted one of the most active terrorist bases in the world. . . . Our forces also attacked a factory in Sudan associated with the bin Laden network. The factory was involved in the production of materials for chemical weapons." At: www.pbs.org/newshour/bb/military/july-dec98/clinton2_8-20.html.

92. "The Mideast Turmoil: Airstrike; Israel Attacks What It Calls a Terrorist Camp in Syria," *New York Times*, October 6, 2003, at; www

.un.org/apps/news/story.asp?NewsID=8452&Cr=Palestin&Cr1=&
Kw1=Security+Council&Kw2=&Kw3=. In June 1994, Israel bombed
the Hezbollah Party of God training camp in Lebanon. "Dozens Are
Killed As Israelis Attack Camp in Lebanon," *New York Times*, June 3,
1994, at: http://query.nytimes.com/gst/fullpage.html?res=9A07E1DD
1E3BF930A35755C0A962958260. Statement by Israeli Defense Minister Rabin on the attack of the PLO base in Tunis on October 1, 1985:
"For a long time now, we have been aware of, have felt the effort of the
terrorist organizations—first and foremost the terrorist organizations
of the PLO headed by Arafat—to carry out attacks from everywhere
and anywhere that Israelis or Israeli targets are to be found: In Israel
and abroad. As long as PLO terrorism, or any other terrorism operates against Israel, Israel will fight against it. Israel will determine the
manner of combat and the site of the attack in accordance with its
own considerations exclusively. The target this time was not personnel directly involved with operations, but the headquarters that decides, plans and directs the attacks, whether from the north or in the
administered areas or from the sea, and against Israelis, such as the
abhorrent murder of the three Israelis in Larnaca." 92 Press Conference Following Israel Air Force Attack on PLO base in Tunis, October
1, 1985, Israeli Ministry of Foreign Affairs. At: www.mfa.gov.il/MFA/
Foreign%20Relations/Israels%20Foreign%20Relations%20since%20
1947/1984-1988/92%20Press%20Conference%20Following%20
Israel%20Air%20Force%20Att.

93. See SC Res. 520 (1982).
94. The Security Council passed Resolution 573, condemning the Israeli
attacks against Tunis on October 4, 1985, with fourteen votes in favor,
and the U.S. abstaining.
95. Syria also presented a draft resolution to the Security Council to condemn the attack on Syrian soil, but after debate no vote was taken.
"The Mideast Turmoil: United Nations; Syria Offers A Resolution To
Condemn Israeli Raid," *New York Times*, October 6, 2003, at: www
.nytimes.com/2003/10/06/world/mideast-turmoil-united-nations-syria-
offers-resolution-condemn-israeli-raid.html?scp=2&sq=The%20
Mideast%20Turmoil:%20United%20Nations;%20Syria%20Offers%
20A%20Resolution%20To%20Condemn%20Israeli%20Raid&st=cse.

96. "The Sudan Airstrike Mystery," *New York Times*, March 26, 2009, at: http://thelede.blogs.nytimes.com/2009/03/26/sudan-airstrike-mystery/?scp=1&sq=%93Israel%20hits%20every%20place% 20it%20can%20in%20order%20to%20stop%20terror,%20near%20and %20far.%94%20&st=cse. See also "U.S. Officials Say Israel Struck in Sudan," *New York Times*, March 26, 2009, at: www.nytimes.com/ 2009/03/27/world/africa/27sudan.html?scp=2&sq=israel%20air%20 strike%20sudan&st=cse.

97. *Corfu Channel (United Kingdom v. Albania)* ICJ, 1949 (para. 177).

98. See *Democratic Republic of the Congo (DRC) v. Uganda*, ICJ, December 19, 2005 (para. 146):

> "146. It is further to be noted that, while Uganda claimed to have acted in self-defence, it did not ever claim that it had been subjected to an armed attack by the armed forces of the DRC. The 'armed attacks' to which reference was made came rather from the ADF. The Court has found above (paragraphs 131–135) that there is no satisfactory proof of the involvement in these attacks, direct or indirect, of the Government of the DRC. The attacks did not emanate from armed bands or irregulars sent by the DRC or on behalf of the DRC, within the sense of Article 3 *(g)* of General Assembly resolution 3314 (XXIX) on the definition of aggression, adopted on 14 December 1974. The Court is of the view that, on the evidence before it, even if this series of deplorable attacks could be regarded as cumulative in character, they still remained non-attributable to the DRC."

99. Id., Para. 303.

100. Id., Para. 147.

101. Franck, pp. 63–64.

102. The Turkish raid against the Kurdistan Workers' Party (a group listed as a terrorist organization by the U.S., the EU, and Turkey) began on December 16, 2006, after October 2006 attacks on Turkish soldiers. Government spokesman for Iraq, Ali al-Dabbagh, said: "Our position is Turkey should respect the sovereignty of Iraq and avoid any military action which would threaten security and stability." Turkey relied on Security Council Resolution 1373, which requires States to control their territory, as a basis for "hot pursuit" of the rebels. "Iraq protests

Turkish incursion into Northern Iraq," *Reuters*, February 22, 2008, at: www.reuters.com/article/gc05/idUSL2281538020080222?sp=true.

103. The only country to support Colombia's actions in the OAS was the U.S., despite FARC having been designated as a terrorist organization by the U.S., Colombia, Canada, and the EU. "Regional Block Criticizes Colombia Raid in Ecuador," *New York Times*, March 6, 2008, at: www.nytimes.com/2008/03/06/world/americas/06venez.html?scp=1&sq=columbia+ecuador+FARC&st=nyt. In CP/RES. 930 (1632/08) (March 5, 2008) the OAS resolved: "To reaffirm the principle that the territory of a state is inviolable and may not be the object, even temporarily, of military occupation or of other measures of force taken by another State, directly or indirectly, on any grounds whatsoever." On March 17, 2008, in RC.25/RES.1/08, the OAS resolved: "To reject the incursion by Colombian military forces and police personnel into the territory of Ecuador, in the Province of Sucumbíos, on March 1, 2008, carried out without the knowledge or prior consent of the Government of Ecuador, since it was a clear violation of Articles 19 and 21 of the OAS Charter." Colombia's Defense Minister, Juan Manuel Santos, called the raid "legitimate defence." *The Economist*, March 7, 2009. See Marcella, Gabriel, *War Without Borders: The Colombia-Ecuador Crisis of 2008* (Strategic Studies Institute, Washington, D.C., 2008).

104. *Case Concerning Armed Activities on the Territory of the Congo (Democratic Republic of the Congo v. Uganda)*, ICJ (December 19, 2005), Para. 146: "while Uganda claimed to have acted in self-defence, it did not ever claim that it had been subjected to an armed attack by the armed forces of the DRC . . . there is no satisfactory proof of the involvement in these attacks, direct or indirect, of the Government of the DRC." Therefore, the ICJ found (Para. 147) "that the legal and factual circumstances for the exercise of a right of self-defence by Uganda against the DRC were not present."

105. See the speech of President Harry S. Truman, "The Truman Doctrine," delivered before a Joint Session of Congress, March 12, 1949, at University of Virginia Miller Center of Public Affairs, at: http://millercenter.org/scripps/archive/speeches/detail/3343.

106. Weisburd, pp. 184–86.

107. Id. at 187–88.

108. Id. at 196–97.

109. "The Buck Stops Here," *New York Times*, July 19, 1987, at: http://www
.nytimes.com/1987/07/19/weekinreview/the-buck-stops-here.html?
scp=31&sq=&pagewanted=all.

110. *Nicaragua v. United States of America*, Merits Judgment, *I.C.J.* (June
27, 1986), p. 237.

111. "El Salvador Halts Ties to Nicaragua," *New York Times*, November 23, 1989, at: www.nytimes.com/1989/11/27/world/el-salvador-
halts-ties-to-nicaragua.html?scp=1&sq=Nicaragua%20El%20
Salvador%20cache%20weapons&st=cse.

112. See generally Holloway, David, "Deterrence, Preventive War and Pre-
emption," in Bunn, George & Chyba, Christopher, eds., *U.S. Nuclear
Weapons Policy: Confronting Today's Threats* (Brookings Institution
Press, Washington, D.C., 2006), pp. 34–74.

113. The Cuban Missile Crisis: Transcript of a Meeting at the White
House, 16 October 1962, at: http://avalon.law.yale.edu/20th_century/
msc_cuba018.asp.

114. For review of the initial announcement (1993) and withdrawal (2003)
of North Korea from the NPT, see "Text of North Korea's Statement
on NPT Withdrawal," James Martin Center for Nonproliferation
Studies, January 10, 2003, at: http://cns.miis.edu/archive/country_
north_korea/nptstate.htm.

115. *CRS Report for Congress*, "North Korea's Nuclear Test: Motivations,
Implications, and U.S. Options" (October 24, 2006). "According to
most informed observers, North Korea does not now have the capability to marry nuclear warheads with long-range missiles. . . ." See
generally Pinkston, Daniel E., "The North Korean Ballistic Missile
Program," *Strategic Studies Institute* (2008).

116. Carter, Ashton B. & Perry, William J., "Nuclear over North Korea:
Back to the Brink," *The Washington Post*, October 20, 2002, at: www
.washingtonpost.com/ac2/wp-dyn?pagename=article&node=&
contentId=A50658-2002Oct19&notFound=true.

117. Wit, Joel S., et al., *Going Critical: The First North Korean Nuclear Crisis*
(Brookings Institution Press, Washington, D.C., 2004), pp. 180–181.

118. The Six Party Talks, between South Korea, North Korea, China, Russia, Japan, and the United States began in August 2003, with the goal
of denuclearizing the Korean Peninsula. During the Fourth Round of
the Talks, the participants released a Joint Statement in which North

Korea agreed to give up its nuclear weapons in exchange for energy assistance, specifically 2 million kilowatts of power from the ROK. At: http://fpc.state.gov/documents/organization/47809.pdf. North Korea tested a nuclear missile on October 9, 2006, but the launch was a failure. The Six Party Talks resumed thereafter but stalled in December 2008. In April 2009 North Korea launched a missile, expelled UN weapons inspectors, and announced that it would resume its nuclear program.

119. North Korea released a statement in response to the debate about intercepting vessels, stating that the DPRK will "regard any hostile actions against the DPRK, including checkup and inspection of its peaceful vessels, as an unpardonable encroachment on the DPRK's sovereignty and counter them with prompt and strong military strikes." "KPA Panmunjom Mission Clarifies Revolutionary Armed Forces' Principled Stand," Korean Central News Agency of DPRK via Korea News Service (KNS), May 27, 2009, at: www.globalsecurity.org/wmd/library/news/dprk/2009/dprk-090527-kcna01.htm. Security Council Resolution 1784 (June 12, 2009) authorized (but did not require) States to prevent North Korea from shipping or otherwise transferring WMD technology or materials. See also SC Resolution 1718 (2006).

120. Katz, Samuel, *Soldier Spies: Israeli Military Intelligence* (Presidio Press, Novato, Calif., 1994), p. 281; Institute for National Security Studies, May 1995, at: www.au.af.mil/auawcawcgate/mcnair41/41irq.htm.

121. Yoo, John, "Using Force," 71 *U. Chi. L. Rev.* 729, 765 (2004).

122. "A Strike in the Dark: Why Did Israel Bomb Syria?" by Seymour Hersh, *The New Yorker*, February 11, 2008. On October 1, 2007, the Syrian Foreign Minister asked the General Assembly to condemn the Israeli attack, stating: "We reiterate that the failure of the international community, including the Security Council, to condemn this act of aggression would encourage Israel to persist in this hostile pursuit, and lead to an exacerbation of tensions in the region." He went on to charge the U.S. with spreading rumors to support Israel's actions. "Syrian Foreign Minister says Security Council should condemn Israeli acts" UN News Centre, October 1, 2007, at: www.un.org/apps/news/story.asp?NewsID=24099&Cr=general&Cr1=debate&Kw1=israel&Kw2=syria&Kw3=.

123. Barletta, Michael, "Chemical Weapons in Sudan: Allegations and Evidence," *The Nonproliferation Review*, Fall 1998, p. 118.

124. Remarks to the United Nations Security Council by Secretary Colin L. Powell, February 5, 2003, in reference to Security Council Res. 1441, calling on Iraq to disarm. At: www.state.gov/documents/organization/20124.pdf. On February 25, 2003, British Prime Minister Tony Blair addressed the House of Commons to the same effect. At: www.publications.parliament.uk/pa/cm200203/cmhansrd/vo030225/debtext/30225-05.htm#30225-05_head0.

125. "Bush Outlines Iraq Threat," Office of the White House Press Secretary, October 7, 2002: "Failure to act would embolden other tyrants, allow terrorists access to new weapons and new resources, and make blackmail a permanent feature of world events. The United Nations would betray the purpose of its founding, and prove irrelevant to the problems of our time." At: http://georgewbush-whitehouse.archives.gov/news/releases/2002/10/20021007-8.html

126. Libya received equipment and "technical training" on nuclear capabilities from Argentina pursuant to a 1974 cooperation treaty. In the early 1980s, Qadafi sought help with production from the USSR, China, and Pakistan, while denying any intention to develop nuclear weapons. For an overview of the Libyan weapons development program, see: www.globalsecurity.org/wmd/world/libya/nuclear.htm. In December 2003, Libya announced that it was terminating its previously denied nuclear weapons program, and claimed that it had cooperated with North Korea in developing long-range Scud missiles and supplied parts to Saddam Hussein's regime. "Bush Official: Libya's Nuclear Program a Surprise," *CNN*, December 19, 2003, at: www.cnn.com/2003/WORLD/africa/12/19/libya.nuclear/index.html.

127. For an overview of A.Q. Khan's involvement in the Libyan nuclear arms development program, see: "Chronology: A.Q. Kahn," *New York Times*, April 16, 2006, at: www.nytimes.com/2006/04/16/world/asia/16chron-khan.html?pagewanted=2&_r=1&sq=libya%20bbc%20china%20khan&st=cse&scp=1.

128. See letter submitted by Ahmed A. Own, Chargé D'affaires of the Permanent Mission of the Libyan Arab Jamahiriya, to the United Nations on August 15, 2003 (S/2003/818): "Libya as a sovereign State: Has

facilitated the bringing to justice of the two suspects charged with the bombing of Pan Am 103 and accepts responsibility for the actions of its officials." Letter available at: www.undemocracy.com/S-2003-818. pdf. Subsequently, the Security Council passed Resolution 1506 lifting the sanctions imposed on Libya (December 9, 2003). Resolution available at: www.un.org/Docs/sc/unsc_resolutions03.html.

129. Iran claims it has no intention to acquire nuclear weapons, and a National Intelligence Estimate (NIE) issued in November 2007 found with a high degree of certainty that Iran ended its program to build nuclear weapons in 2003. Iran has, however, continued to pursue the ability to enrich uranium, which is the single most important capacity it needs to make nuclear weapons, and the NIE confirmed that Iran still most probably intends to acquire such weapons:

"(A) We judge with high confidence that in fall 2003, Tehran halted its nuclear weapons program; we also assess with moderate-to-high confidence that Tehran at a minimum is keeping open the option to develop nuclear weapons. . . . We assess with moderate confidence Tehran had not restarted its nuclear weapons program as of mid-2007, but we do not know whether it currently intends to develop nuclear weapons. . . . (C) We assess centrifuge enrichment is how Iran probably could first produce enough fissile material for a weapon, if it decides to do so. Iran resumed its declared centrifuge enrichment activities in January 2006, despite the continued halt in the nuclear weapons program. . . . (D) Iran's civilian uranium enrichment program is continuing. We also assess with high confidence that since fall 2003, Iran has been conducting research and development projects with commercial and conventional military applications—some of which would also be of limited use for nuclear weapons."

The National Intelligence Estimate: "Key Judgments: Iran: Nuclear Intelligence and Capabilities" is available at: www.dni.gov/.

130. Iran's call for the destruction of Israel must be taken into account in evaluating the risk posed if it were actually to acquire nuclear weapons; yet, Iran insists it has no intention to attack Israel. In a speech by President Mahmoud Ahmadinejad to an Islamic Student Associations conference on "The World without Zionism" on October 26,

2005, he said the following: "Our dear Imam said that the occupying regime must be wiped off the map and this was a very wise statement. We cannot compromise over the issue of Palestine. Is it possible to create a new front in the heart of an old front? This would be a defeat and whoever accepts the legitimacy of this regime [Israel] has in fact, signed the defeat of the Islamic world." "Text of Mahmoud Ahmadinejad's Speech," *New York Times*, October 30, 2005, at: www .nytimes.com/2005/10/30/weekinreview/30iran.html?pagewanted= 1&ei=5070&en=26f07fc5b7543417&ex=1161230400. Soon after the media picked up this call to wipe Israel off the map, the speech was removed from the Iranian Student News Association Web site, and President Ahmadinejad insisted that Iran has no plan to attack Israel. "Iran 'not planning Israel attack'," *BBC News*, October 29, 2005, at: http://news.bbc.co.uk/2/hi/middle_east/4387852.stm.

131. "Gates warns against Israeli strike on Iran's nuclear facilities," *Los Angeles Times*, April 16, 2009, at: www.latimes.com/news/nationworld/ world/la-fg-us-iran16-2009apr16,0,5208507.story.

132. Bolton, John, "What if Israel Strikes Iran?" *Wall Street Journal*, June 12, 2009, at: http://online.wsj.com/article/SB124467678369503997.html.

133. The "Blood Telegram" circulated in the U.S. State Department condemning the genocide in East Pakistan is available at: www.gwu.edu/ ~nsarchiv/NSAEBB/NSAEBB79/BEBB8.pdf. Security Council Resolution 307, calling for an immediate cessation of hostilities between India and Pakistan (December 21, 1971), is available at: www.global policy.org/security/issues/ind-pak/resolutions/1971res.pdf.

134. Franck, pp. 143–45. For an overview of the 1978–79 Uganda-Tanzania conflict, see Burmester, Byron F., "Comment: On Humanitarian Intervention: The New World Order and Wars to Preserve Human Rights," *Utah L. Rev.* 269 (1994). An effort by Tanzania in 1972 to assist in the overthrow of Amin, generated by Amin's claims and incursions into Tanzanian territory, was unsuccessful. Weisburd, pp. 197–98.

135. "Vietnam's Vietnam: Scars of Cambodia," *New York Times*, April 9, 1989, at: www.nytimes.com/1989/04/09/world/vietnam-s-vietnam-scars-of-cambodia.html?scp=6&sq=vietnam%20and%20cambodia% 20and%20border%20and%201978%20and%20Pol%20Pot&st=cse.

136. Norway concurred with France: "The Norwegian Government and

public opinion in Norway have expressed strong objections to the serious violations of human rights committed by the Pol Pot Government. However, the domestic policies of that Government cannot—
we repeat, cannot—justify the actions of Vietnam over the last days
and weeks. The Norwegian Government firmly rejects the threat or
use of force against the territorial integrity or political independence
of any State. At: www.idrc.ca/openebooks/963-1/-ch4fn94." Like-
wise, Poland stated: "Neither do we have any doubt about the ap-
palling record of violation of the most basic and elementary human
rights in Kampuchea. . . . [Nonetheless], there are no, nor can there
be any, socio-political considerations that would justify the invasion
of the territory of a sovereign State by the forces of another State."
Singapore stated: "It has been said by others that the Government of
Democratic Kampuchea has treated its people in a barbarous fash-
ion. Whether that accusation is true or false is not the issue before
the Council. . . . No other country has a right to topple the Government of Democratic Kampuchea, however badly that Government
may have treated its people. At: www.idrc.ca/openebooks/963-1/
-ch4fn99." *The Responsibility to Protect: Supplementary Volume to
The Report of The International Commission on Intervention and State
Sovereignty* (International Development Research Centre, Ottawa,
Ontario, 2001). Supplementary report available at: www.idrc.ca/
openebooks/963-1/.

137. Wesiburd, pp. 42–44.
138. The Central African Republic became independent in 1960, but had
     strong historical ties with France. After the country verged on bank-
     ruptcy, Jean-Bedel Bokassa took the presidency from David Dacko in
     a coup, and renamed the country the Central African Empire, and
     himself president for life. France decided to take action after the mas-
     sacre of school children in 1979. For a brief history of the Central Af-
     rican Republic, see: http://news.bbc.co.uk/1/hi/world/africa/1067615
     .stm.
139. "The World: When Empires Fall, Not Everyone Emerges With a
     State of His Own," *New York Times*, April 14, 1991, at: www.nytimes
     .com/1991/04/14/weekinreview/the-world-when-empires-fall-not-
     everyone-emerges-with-a-state-of-his-own.html?n=Top/Reference/
     Times%20Topics/Subjects/I/Immigration%20and%20Refugees&

scp=6&sq=1991%20iraq%20kurd%20april%20britain%20france%20 36th%20parallel&st=cse.

140. "After the War; U.S. Presses Iraq to Accept U.N. Force to Protect Kurds," *New York Times*, May 11, 1991, at: www.nytimes.com/1991/ 05/11/world/after-the-war-us-presses-iraq-to-accept-un-force-to-protect-kurds.html?scp=1&sq=China%20veto%20resolution%20 security%20council%20intervention%20iraq%201991&st=cse.

141. "Containment: The Iraqi no-fly zones," *BBC News*, December 29, 1998, at: http://news.bbc.co.uk/2/hi/eventscrisis_in_the_gulf/forces_and _firepower/244364.stm.

142. *New York Times*, October 15, 1994, p. A1.

143. See Peter A. Jenkins, "The Economic Community of West African States and the Regional Use of Force," 35 *Denv. J. Int'l L. & Pol'y* 333 (2007).

144. "Decisions Adopted by the Sixty-Sixth Ordinary Session of the Council of Ministers," Organization of African Unity, May 28–31, 1997, p. 29, available at: www.africa-union.org/root/au/Documents/ Decisions/com/47CoM_1997b.pdf.

145. "Statement by the President of the Security Council," (S/PRST/1997/ 36) 11 July 1997, available at: www.securitycouncilreport.org/atf/ cf/%7B65BFCF9B-6D27-4E9C-8CD3-CF6E4FF96FF9%7D/Chap% 20VII%20PRST%201997%2036.pdf.

146. Levitt, Jeremy I., "Illegal Peace?: An Inquiry into the Legality of Power-Sharing with Warlords and Rebels in Africa," 27 *Mich. J. Int'l L.* 495 (2006). See also Security Council Res. 1132 (1997) establishing travel sanctions against the military junta and an oil embargo; available at: http://daccessdds.un.org/doc/UNDOC/GEN/N97/267/13/ PDF/N9726713.pdf?OpenElement.

147. "Statement made by Acting President, Dr. MG Buthelezi, on Lesotho, National Assembly," South African Government Information, September 22, 1998, at: www.info.gov.za/speeches/1998/98925_buthel 9811144.htm; "Lesotho Votes for Legislators Under a System New to Africa," *New York Times*, May 26, 2002, at: www.nytimes.com/ 2002/05/26/world/lesotho-votes-for-legislators-under-a-system-new-to-africa.html?scp=9&sq=lesotho%20election%20coup&st=cse.

148. SCOR (LIV), 3989th Meeting, March 26, 1999, at p. 6.

149. See Thomas, Juma, "Tanzania to send 750 soldiers to Comoros," *IPP Media*, March 15, 2008, at: www.ippmedia.com/cgi-bin/ipp/print.pl? id=110416; Kato, Levina, "Comoros: Raid to Proceed, Says Tanzania," *Daily Nation on the Web*, March 18, 2008, at: http://allafrica.com/stories/200803180148.html.

150. The number of people killed in the Rwandan genocide is still debated, with the figure usually estimated at 800,000. However, the U.S. State Department put the figure closer to one million killed. See report at: www.state.gov/r/pa/ho/pubs/8531.htm.

151. The Council on Foreign Relations, Center for Preventive Action report (released October 2008) "Congo: Securing Peace, Sustaining Progress" estimates that two and a half million Congolese died between the start of the civil war in 1998 and general cessation of hostilities in 2001, and that an estimated three million Congolese have died from violence, hunger, and disease since 2001. Report available at: www.cfr.org/content/publications/attachments/Congo_CSR40.pdf.

152. A February 2009 report to the UN Security Council explains that the crisis caused by Mugabe's regime in Zimbabwe has led to a "collapse in recent months of the health, water and sanitation systems. A consequence was the onset of a cholera epidemic that since August has claimed more than 2,800 lives. The World Health Organization indicated that more than 50,000 people have been infected. Over 1,500 new cases emerge daily . . . . [The WHO] described the health situation as a man-made disaster, placed the blame on the Mugabe regime and called for urgent intervention by the UN and Zimbabwe's neighbours to stem the loss of life." Report available at: www.securitycouncilreport.org/site/c.glKWLeMTIsG/b.4916619/k.FA9A/February_2009brZimbabwe.htm.

153. In 1996, the UN reported that the Burundi army killed between 2,100 and 3,000 Hutu civilians. "U.N. Reports Burundi Army Slew Civilians By Thousands," *New York Times*, August 4, 1996, at: www.nytimes.com/1996/08/04/world/un-reports-burundi-army-slew-civilians-by-thousands.html.

154. The UN estimates that more than 200,000 people have been killed in the Darfur region of Sudan and over 2 million people displaced since fighting broke out in 2003. In 2007 a joint peacekeeping op-

eration between the UN and the African Union entered Sudan. See the UN Fact Sheet on the Darfur Genocide, at: http://www.un.org/News/dh/infocus/sudan/fact_sheet.pdf. The Sudanese President, Omar Al Bashir, was charged with war crimes and crimes against humanity by the International Criminal Court's Prosecutor on March 4, 2009. See overview of charges at: www.icc-cpi.int/Menus/ICC/Situations+and+Cases/Situations/Situation+ICC+0205/.

155. The cyber attack consisted of taking control of computers around the globe to direct massive amounts of data at Estonian Web sites. It nearly shut down the Internet in Estonia, froze many government Web sites, and shut down the Web site of the largest bank in the country, causing an estimated $1 million in losses. "Digital Fears Emerge After Data Siege in Estonia," *New York Times*, May 29, 2007, at: www.nytimes.com/2007/05/29/technology/29estonia.html?pagewanted=1&sq=estonia%20cyber%20attack&st=nyt&scp=1.

156. "U.S. Plans Attack and Defense in Web Warfare," *New York Times*, April 28, 2009, pp. A1, 14, col. 3.

157. The Computer Crime and Security Survey 2007, previously developed with the FBI, with the most recent survey conducted solely by the CSI, is available at: www.gocsi.com/press/20070913.jhtml. The survey reports that, "in total, 194 responses yielded losses of $66,930,950 (see figure 16), up from $52,494,290 (for 313 respondents) in 2006."

158. "Intel director: Iran, cyber threats biggest worry." *MSNBC*, January 16, 2009, at: www.msnbc.msn.com/id/28699004/.

159. A 2001 Convention on Cybercrime developed by the Council of Europe calls for signatories to establish jurisdiction over various cybercrimes. Convention on Cybercrime, The Council of Europe, January 23, 2001, available at: http://conventions.coe.int/Treaty/Commun/QueVoulezVous.asp?NT=185&CL=ENG. The Draft International Convention to Enhance Protection from Cyber Crime and Terrorism goes much further, calling for jurisdiction over a broader array of cyber crimes and the establishment of an international agency to develop transnational policies for effective regulation under private-sector control. Sofaer, Abraham D. & Goodman, Seymour E., eds., *The Transnational Dimension of Cyber Crime and Terrorism* (Hoover Institution Press, Stanford, Calif., 2001), pp. 249–265.

160. "New Military Command to Focus on Cybersecurity," *Wall Street Journal*, April 22, 2009, at: http://online.wsj.com/article/SB12403573 8674441033.html.

161. Owens, William A., Dam, Kenneth W., & Lin, Herbert S., eds., *Technology, Policy, Law, and Ethics Regarding U.S. Acquisition and Use of Cyberattack Capabilities* (National Academies Press, Washington, D.C., 2009), p. S-5.

162. The NRC Report concludes that "enduring unilateral dominance with respect to cyber conflict is not realistically achievable by the United States (or any other nation)." Id. at 11–18.

163. See "Security Council Hears over 60 Speakers in Two-Day Debate on Iraq's Disarmament; Many Say Use of Force should be Last Resort, Others Urge Swift Action," February 19, 2003, at: www.un.org/News/Press/docs/2003/sc7666.doc.htm.

Chapter 5

1. James Steinberg, currently deputy secretary of state, wrote in his paper "The Use of Preventive Force as an Element of US National Strategy" that "the threat of preventive strikes may help to deter the potential acquirer from pursuing the dangerous capability, or lead them to the negotiating table, as with the North Koreans in 1994." Paper available at: www.princeton.edu/~ppns/papers/Steinberg_Preemption.pdf.

2. The 1998 bombing of Al Shifa pharmaceutical factory is still protested by the Sudanese government; the U.S. has not apologized for the bombing. "Look at the Place! Sudan Says, 'Say Sorry,' but U.S. Won't," *New York Times*, October 20, 2005, at: www.nytimes.com/2005/10/20/international/africa/20khartoum.html?_r=1.

3. The Islamist group Tehrik-e-Taliban, led by Baitullah Mehsud, warned that it would respond to U.S. missile attacks and increased Pakistan armed forces operations. It has reportedly done so by conducting bombings and other assaults in Lahore and other urban centers. See "Militant Claims Responsibility for Pakistan Attack," *New York Times*, March 31, 2009, at: www.nytimes.com/2009/04/01/world/asia/01pstan.html.

4. President Eisenhower outlined some of the dangers of atomic war with the Soviet Union in his December 8, 1953, speech entitled "Atoms for Peace," given before the UN General Assembly on the topic of Peaceful

Uses of Atomic Energy. Among his points are statements implying the U.S. has no desire to control the USSR, or to launch a preventive attack that includes nuclear weapons: "My country wants to be constructive, not destructive. It wants agreement, not wars, among nations. It wants itself to live in freedom, and in the confidence that the people of every other nation enjoy equally the right of choosing their own way of life . . . salvation cannot be attained by one dramatic act." Available at: www.iaea.org/About/history_speech.html.

5. See Kellman, Barry, "Responses to the September 11 Attacks: An International Criminal Law Approach to Bioterrorism," 25 *Harv. J.L. & Pub. Policy* 721 (2002): "The ease with which pathogens can be carried or shipped means that unilateral action cannot prevent bioterrorism. Investigators may uncover a secret laboratory in the United States, but a laboratory in most other parts of the world could easily escape detection, and operations could proceed with minimal risk. Robust domestic regulatory and law enforcement capabilities alone would have negligible ability to detect foreign terrorists who are developing biological agents nor to prevent someone from bringing weaponized agents to the United States." Later, Kellman states: "Biological weapons can also be inflicted discreetly, enabling terrorists to flee after an attack, but before law enforcement personnel are on full alert. The important point here is that disarmament and non-proliferation measures are likely to be inapposite for addressing biological weapons threats—a control strategy that does not focus on terrorist acquisition and use of biological weapons is wrongly directed . . . capabilities for producing biological weapons are ubiquitous, but capabilities for verifying their non-production are illusory. Any reasonably equipped biological research laboratory or bio-pharmaceutical facility has the capacity to make biological weapons quickly and, just as quickly, to eliminate any trace of that activity."

6. By preparing for a pandemic, countries will simultaneously prepare against bioterrorism events: "WHO Guidelines on the Use of Vaccines and Antivirals during Influenza Pandemics." The WHO emphasizes that "countries will be able to address pandemic requirements only if they plan for supplies of vaccines and antivirals now." See report at: www.wpro.who.int/NR/rdonlyres/263D6E1A-49B9-4824-B671-A86 45096EC13/0/11_29_01_A.pdf. Special emphasis in bioterrorism

defense is being given to preparing vaccines and medications for small-pox, anthrax, influenza, and the plague.

7. Weapons could be detected with Chemical and Biological Mass Spectrometers. See overview of capabilities at: www.ornl.gov/sci/engineering_science_technology/sms/Hardy%20Fact%20Sheets/Block%20II.pdf.

8. See "Bioterrorism Information for First Responders" available at the Centers for Disease Control and Prevention: www.bt.cdc.gov/bioterrorism/responders.asp.

9. See the review of dangers involved in interventions in Coady, C.A.J. (Tony), "Intervention, Political Realism and the Ideal of Peace," in Coady, Tony & Michael O'Keefe, *Righteous Violence: The Ethics and Politics of Military Intervention* (Melbourne Univ. Press, Melbourne, Australia, 2005), pp. 14–31.

Chapter 6

1. Kissinger, Henry, *Diplomacy* (Simon and Schuster, New York, 1995), pp. 249–50: "During the Cold War, the United Nations proved . . . ineffective in every case involving Great Power aggression, due to either the communist veto in the Security Council or the reluctance on the part of smaller countries to run risks on behalf of issues they felt did not concern them . . . The United Nations . . . failed to fulfill the underlying premise of collective security—the prevention of war and collective resistance to aggression."

2. See Doyle, Michael W., *Striking First: Preemption and Prevention in International Conflict* (Princeton Univ. Press, Princeton, N.J., 2008), pp. 7–10.

3. On December 11, 1992, the Security Council passed Resolution 795 "to establish a presence of the United Nations Protection Force" in Macedonia. The resolution is available at: http://www.nato.int/ifor/un/u921211a.htm. The UNPROFOR was reestablished as the UN Preventive Deployment force. Ludlow, David J. "Preventive peacemaking in Macedonia: An assessment of U.N. good offices diplomacy," *B.Y.U.L. Rev.* 761 (2003).

4. *The National Security Strategy of the United States of America* (September 2002), pp. 13–16, at: www.state.gov/documents/organization/15538.pdf; *The National Security Strategy of the United States of*

America (March 2006), pp. 18–23, at: www.strategicstudiesinstitute
.army.mil/pdffiles/nss.pdf.

5. The Report adds (p. 10): "It is a condition of a rule-based international
order that law evolves in response to developments such as proliferation, terrorism and global warming."

6. For example, the Bishkek Statement among the Republic of Kazakh-
stan, the People's Republic of China, the Kyrgyz Republic, the Russian
Federation, and the Republic of Tajikistan, released August 25, 1999,
states the following goal: "strengthening the role of the United Nations
as the basic mechanism for safeguarding world peace and tranquility
and peaceful settlement of international and regional issues and op-
posing the use of force and threat to use force in international relations
without the approval of the UN Security Council." Source: *Beijing Review*, Vol. 42 No. 37, September 13, 1999.

7. The 2003 invasion of Iraq led the French Prime Minister to state to the
National Assembly: "France is relying on the United Nations and refusing unilateralism . . . . [A] war would rock the international order by
undermining collective security and multilateralism, by the primacy
accorded to the doctrine of pre-emptive action over the principle of
legitimate defense." (February 26, 2003) Germany, Norway, Croatia,
and others have rejected preventive actions and unilateralism. See also
Netherlands Advisory Council on International Law, Report on Preemptive Action, No. 36, July 2004 (p. 20): "The US National Security
Strategy also appears to be inconsistent with the principle that the Security Council is the sole body that is entitled to determine the existence
of any threat to international peace and security under Article 39 of the
UN Charter and, accordingly, that it is the Security Council which is
obliged to take the necessary action." This report was requested by the
Dutch government as guidance on the political and military desirability of or need for preemptive action. On the other hand, some European
states support unilateral action when multilateral action is not possible.
Russia's Chief of Staff, General Yury Baluyevsky, stated on September
8, 2004, after the Beslan school massacre that Russia will act to preempt
strikes if its security is threatened, but will resort to nuclear weapons
only if the country's very existence is threatened. Speech available at:
http://web.lexis-nexis.com/universe/document?_m=39f7121861bc70
c83e9575fdac00d49f&_docnum=85&wchp=dGLbVtb-zSkVA&_md5

=3a3a42645bfaadacfd01876b05c8f02. Prime Minister Tony Blair has stated that when a security threat is clear, such as terrorists obtaining WMD, "our duty" is "to act to eliminate it." "[W]e surely have a duty and a right to prevent the threat materializing . . ." Statement available at: www.pm.gov.uk/output.Page5461.asp. See also, Netherlands Advisory Council on International Law, *Report on Pre-emptive Action*, No. 36, July 2004 (p. 20): "The US National Security Strategy also appears to be inconsistent with the principle that the Security Council is the sole body that is entitled to determine the existence of any threat to international peace and security under Article 39 of the UN Charter and, accordingly, that it is the Security Council which is obliged to take the necessary action." This report was requested by the Dutch government as guidance on the political and military desirability of or need for preemptive action.

8. According to the Protocol of the Peace and Security Council of the African Union, Art. 13.3c–d, the AU is allowed "intervention in a Member State in respect of grave circumstances or at the request of a Member State in order to restore peace and security, in accordance with Article 4(h) and (j) of the Constitutive Act; d. preventive deployment in order to prevent (i) a dispute or a conflict from escalating, (ii) an ongoing violent conflict from spreading to neighboring areas or States, and (iii) the resurgence of violence after parties to a conflict have reached an agreement." Protocol available at: www.africa-union .org/root/AU/Documents/Treaties/Text/Protocol_peace%20and%20 security.pdf.

9. Charter of the OAS, Ch. IV, Art. 19.

10. Asian States are especially resistant to UN intrusions into domestic matters. See Shulong, Chu, "China, Asia and Issues of Sovereignty and Intervention," Academy of International Studies and Department of International Relations, Nankai University, Pugwash Occasional Papers Vol. 2, No. 1 (2001). At: www.irchina.org/en/xueren/china/view .asp?id=808.

11. Res. 1373, adopted September 28, 2001. "Security Council Unanimously Adopts Wide-Ranging Anti-Terrorism Resolution; Calls for Suppressing Financing, Improving International Cooperation." Resolution available at: www.un.org/News/Press/docs/2001/sc7158.doc .htm. The Security Council has condemned serious violations of

human rights in resolutions aimed at specific States, and it has noted the Universal Declaration of Human Rights in several resolutions, including Res. 1624, S/8586, and Res. 182. In Res. 1540, adopted April 28, 2004, the Council required all States to prevent proliferation of WMD. At: www.un.org/news/Press/docs/2004/sc8076.doc.htm.

12. See High-level Panel report at 23, summarizing the "six clusters of threats with which the world must be concerned now and in the decades ahead," including inter-state conflict, internal conflict (genocide and other atrocities), nuclear, radiological, chemical and biological weapons, terrorism, and transnational organized crime.

13. Resolution 377(V), also known as the Uniting for Peace resolution, allows the General Assembly to meet on matters where the Security Council cannot come to consensus. The Resolution "[r]esolves that if the Security Council, because of lack of unanimity of the permanent members, fails to exercise its primary responsibility for the maintenance of international peace and security in any case where there appears to be a threat to the peace, breach of the peace, or act of aggression, the General Assembly shall consider the matter immediately with a view to making appropriate recommendations to Members for collective measures, including in the case of a breach of the peace or act of aggression the use of armed force when necessary, to maintain or restore international peace and security." Available at: www.un.org/documents/ga/res/5/ares5.htm. This Resolution's history is described in Krasno, Jean & Das, Mitushi, "The Uniting for Peace resolution and other ways of circumventing the authority of the Security Council," in Cronin, Bruce & Hurd, Ian, eds., *The UN Security Council and the Politics of International Authority* (Routledge, London, 2008), pp. 173–95.

14. On November 30, 1973, the International Convention on the Suppression and Punishment of the Crime of Apartheid was adopted in the General Assembly. Under Article I: "The States Parties to the present Convention declare that apartheid is a crime against humanity and that inhuman acts resulting from the policies and practices of apartheid and similar policies and practices of racial segregation and discrimination, as defined in article II of the Convention, are crimes violating the principles of international law, in particular the purposes and principles of the Charter of the United Nations, and constituting a

serious threat to international peace and security." Convention available at: www.unhchr.ch/html/menu3/b/11.htm.

15. The High-level Panel (pp. 87–88) made only the most recent of many proposals to amend the Charter to extend Permanent Security Council membership to major States that contribute significantly to U.N. expenditures from geographic areas not now so represented.

16. HCJ 7957/04, 9 July 2004. 23. "The Advisory Opinion of the International Court of Justice at The Hague determined that the authority to erect the fence is not to be based upon the law of self-defense. The reason for this is that §51 of the Charter of the United Nations recognizes the natural right of self-defense, when one state militarily attacks another state. Since Israel is not claiming that the source of the attack upon her is a foreign state, there is no application of this provision regarding the erection of the wall (paragraph 138 of the Advisory Opinion of the International Court of Justice at The Hague)." Lauterpacht, Elihu, & Greenwood, C.J., *International Law Reports*, Vol. 129 (Cambridge Univ. Press, New York, 2007), p. 262.

17. See *Nicaragua v. United States of America*, Merits: Judgment, International Court of Justice, June 27, 1986, at paragraph 247: "The Court has already indicated (paragraph 238) its conclusion that the conduct of the United States towards Nicaragua cannot be justified by the right of collective self-defence in response to an alleged armed attack on one or other of Nicaragua's neighbours. So far as regards the allegations of supply of arms by Nicaragua to the armed opposition in El Salvador the Court has indicated that while the concept of an armed attack includes the despatch by one State of armed bands into the territory of another State the supply of arms and other support to such bands cannot be equated with armed attack. Nevertheless, such activities may well constitute a breach of the principle of the non-use of force and an intervention in the internal affairs of a State, that is, a form of conduct which is certainly wrongful but is of lesser gravity than an armed attack. The Court must therefore enquire now whether the activities of the United States towards Nicaragua might be justified as a response to an intervention by that State in the internal affairs of another State in Central America." Id. at paragraph 249: "On the legal level the Court cannot regard response to an intervention by Nicaragua as such a justification. While an armed attack would give rise to an entitlement to

collective self-defence, a use of force of a lesser degree of gravity cannot as the Court has already observed (paragraph 211 above) produce any entitlement to take collective countermeasures involving the use of force. The acts of which Nicaragua is accused, even assuming them to have been established and imputable to that State, could only have justified proportionate counter-measures on the part of the State which had been the victim of these acts, namely El Salvador, Honduras or Costa Rica. They could not justify counter-measures taken by a third State, the United States, and particularly could not justify intervention involving the use of force."

18. See Franck, Thomas M., "On Proportionality of Countermeasures in International Law," 102 *A.J.I.L.* 715 (2008), commenting upon *Democratic Republic of the Congo v. Uganda*, Judgment, International Court of Justice, December 19, 2005: "The majority therefore did not think it necessary 'to enquire whether such an entitlement to self-defence was in fact exercised in circumstances of necessity and in a manner that was proportionate' . . . however, the Court chose to make observations on this very point, adding that 'the taking of airports and towns many hundreds of kilometres from Uganda's border would not seem proportionate . . . , nor to be necessary to that end.' Repeating the analytical approach used in *Nicaragua*, the Court employed proportionality in two ways. First, it assessed the right of Uganda to resort to force under Article 51 by reviewing whether it had been the victim of an actual armed attack attributable to the Congo. The majority concluded that no such attack had occurred as would justify Uganda's military response. Controversially, the judges were unwilling to hold the government of the Congo directly responsible for the FUNA's cross-border incursions. Nevertheless, the Court then went on to review the proportionality of Uganda's response. Strictly speaking, these further observations were dicta. Nevertheless, the Court, in both instances, staked out the right to determine, case by case, whether a provocation rises to a threshold permitting the taking of military countermeasures (the *jus ad bellum*). In neither case, however, was that threshold made significantly more determinate by the opinion rendered. While both decisions appear to imply that the provision of sanctuary and support for a cross-border insurgency might potentially rise to the level of an armed attack, justifying a military response, neither offers a

principled rule by which that threshold may be determined in subsequent disputes."

19. Former Legal Advisor to the State Department, Abram Chayes, argued the inherent right of self-defense persists only "until the Security Council has taken the measures necessary to maintain international peace and security." "Perspective on the Persian Gulf: Gulf War isn't possible without the U.N.; the Charter precludes unilateral military action. The realities on the ground bear the same message." *Los Angeles Times*, November 9, 1991. In his view, once the Council assumed jurisdiction over a matter, it alone was competent to act on that issue. Analogous to this argument, though not as extreme, is Professor Christine Gray's criticism of U.S. and Israeli actions claimed to have been taken in self-defense, including the attack on Libya after several terrorist attacks on U.S. nationals: "It is difficult to see how the use of force was necessary, given that the attacks on the nationals had already taken place." Gray, p. 118.

20. Franck, Thomas M., *The Power of Legitimacy Among Nations* (Oxford Univ. Press, New York, 1990), pp. 75–77.

21. See the discussion in Cassese, Antonio, *International Law in a Divided World* (Clarendon Press, Oxford, U.K., 1986), pp. 230–33, concluding that a consensus is growing to permit anticipatory self-defense under strict restrictions related to imminence of an armed attack that would jeopardize the life of the target state and in the absence of peaceful means to prevent it. In his *International Law* (Oxford Univ. Press, New York, 2005) he states (p. 362): "it is more judicious to consider such action as *legally prohibited*, while admittedly knowing that there may be cases where breaches of the prohibition may be justified on moral and political grounds and the community will eventually condone them or mete out lenient condemnation." This description is provided in Malcolm N. Shaw's *International Law* (Cambridge Univ. Press, Cambridge, U.K., 2008), p. 1139 n. 99.

22. The High-level Panel concluded the right to respond to imminent threats is part of established international law. But the notion that "established international law" was preserved in the Charter would permit the argument that the Charter preserves the full scope of the historic right of self-defense. It is to avoid this logical consequence that some prominent scholars have argued that the language of Article 51

prevents all forms of anticipatory uses of force, even those in response to an imminent threat of attack.

23. These words were conveyed by Secretary Webster to British Foreign Secretary Henry Fox following an incident in 1837 in which British authorities in Canada sank a private schooner, *The Caroline*, in U.S. waters because it was being used to carry supplies to insurgents in Canada trying to undermine British authority. The situation was not one in which a State was concerned that another State was preparing to attack or gaining capacities that made it likely that it would some-day attack or help a terrorist group to do so. It was, rather, a situation in which the British government claimed that the U.S. government was either unable or unwilling to stop U.S. supporters of the rebels from assisting them in conducting attacks on Canadian authorities. Webster's dictum was based on the premise that the United States was both able and willing to stop support for the rebels, and that therefore a "reasonable" use of force by British authorities could only occur in the context of a threat so "imminent" that they could not rely on the United States to use its police powers to prevent it. Sofaer, Abraham D., "On the Necessity of Pre-emption," *EJIL* 14 (2003), pp. 212–13.

24. Richter, Chris, "Pre-emptive Self Defense, International Law, and US Policy," *Dialogue* (2003) 1:2, p. 57, quoting from Jennings et al. 1996:420.

25. See generally Sofaer, Abraham D., "International Law and the Use of Force," *The National Interest: International Law & Order* (Transaction Publisher, New Brunswick, N.J., 2003).

26. "European Security Strategy: A Secure Europe in a Better World," adopted on December 12, 2003, p. 7: "Our traditional concept of self-defence—up to and including the Cold War—was based on the threat of invasion. With the new threats, the first line of defence will often be abroad. The new threats are dynamic. The risks of proliferation grow over time; left alone, terrorist networks will become ever more danger-ous. State failure and organised crime spread if they are neglected—as we have seen in West Africa. This implies that we should be ready to act before a crisis occurs. Conflict prevention and threat prevention cannot start too early."

27. Michael J. Glennon argues that legal norms are changing based on State practice: "the gravity of a threat and the probability of its occurrence

weigh far more heavily than a threat's imminence. If a nation is faced with a threat from some rogue state or terrorist group that is both grave and probable, what real-world decision-maker would delay acting until that threat is immediate—until there are no alternatives—until it may be impossible for the state to defend itself?" Glennon, Michael J., "Force and the Settlement of Political Disputes," Debate with Alain Pellet, The Hague Colloquium on Topicality of the 1907 Hague Conference, September 7, 2007. Available at: SSRN: http://ssrn.com/abstract=1092212p.9. Anne-Marie Slaughter and Carl Kaysen adopt the same position: "[A]n intervention in the traditional language of international law is an illegal action. In our exploration of changing legal concepts and evolving norms, this connotation is no longer universally appropriate." See Slaughter, Anne-Marie & Kaysen, Carl, "Introductory Note: Emerging Norms of Justified Intervention," *Emerging Norms of Justified Intervention* (Committee on International Security Studies, Cambridge, Mass., 1993), pp. 7–14.

28. Professor Bruno Simma has stated the majority view, regarding Kosovo as a "hard case" that should not be allowed to make "bad" law. He applauds the German government's view that "the decision of NATO must not become a precedent. As far as the Security Council monopoly on force is concerned, we must avoid getting on a slippery slope." (Quoting from Plenarprotokoll 13/248 (October 16, 1998), at 23129.) What this means is unclear, since Germany and NATO would probably take the same action again in what they considered an identical situation. Simma's explanation is that Kosovo is "a singular case in which NATO decided to act . . . out of overwhelming humanitarian necessity, but from which no general conclusion ought to be drawn." Simma, Bruno, "NATO, the UN and the Use of Force: Legal Aspects: The Threat or Use of Force in International Law," *EJIL* 1999 10(1). Professor Antonio Cassese, a presiding judge of the International Criminal Tribunal for the former Yugoslavia, agreed with Simma that NATO acted illegally in Kosovo, and that its action should not set a precedent. He concluded, however, that the action was justified "from an ethical viewpoint" and cited factors that support this view, noting the possibility that the international community is moving toward a new norm of conduct that creates "an aggravated form of state responsibility" for "large-scale atrocities," permitting forceful intervention. Cassese, Antonio, "Ex iniuria ius oritur: Are We Moving towards International Le-

gitimization of Forcible Humanitarian Countermeasures in the World Community?" 1999 EJIL 10(23). Professor Thomas Franck also denies the legality of the Kosovo intervention while noting that "NATO's action in Kosovo is not the first time illegal steps have been taken to prevent something palpably worse." Franck, Thomas M., "Sidelined in Kosovo? The United Nations' Demise Has Been Exaggerated: Break It, Don't Fake It," *Foreign Affairs* (July/Aug. 1999).

29. See, e.g., Power, Samantha, *A Problem from Hell: America and the Age of Genocide* (Basic Books, New York, 2002); Shawcross, William, *Deliver Us From Evil* (Touchstone, New York, 2000).

30. The recent history of humanitarian intervention prior to the development of the Responsibility to Protect includes declarations primarily by developing countries on culture-specific determinations of human rights and limitations on the right to intervene. See the Tunis Declaration (1992) of the African States meeting at Tunis in preparation for the World Conference on Human Rights, and pursuant to General Assembly resolution 46/111 at 5: "No ready-made model can be prescribed at the universal level since the historical and cultural realities of each nation and the traditions, standards and values of each people cannot be disregarded." See also the Bangkok Declaration (1993), report of the regional meeting for Asia of the World Conference on Human Rights (A/CONF.157/ASRM/8), which stresses "the universality, objectivity, and non-selectivity of all human rights and the need to avoid the application of double standards in the implementation of human rights and its politicization." At 4, the Bangkok Declaration "Discourage(s) any attempt to use human rights as a conditionality for extending development assistance . . . 5. Emphasize(s) the principles of respect for national sovereignty and territorial integrity as well as non-interference in the internal affairs of States, and the non-use of human rights as an instrument of political pressure . . . 8. Recognize(s) that while human rights are universal in nature, they must be considered in the context of dynamic and evolving process of international norm-setting, bearing in mind the significance of national and regional particularities and various historical, cultural, and religious backgrounds."

31. A comprehensive and objective account of humanitarian intervention is provided in Simons, Penelope C., "Humanitarian Intervention: A Review of Literature," Ploughshares Working Paper 01–? (Ploughshares),

including a reference to scholars who do not agree that a consensus has developed in favor of a right of humanitarian intervention, even with U.N. Security Council approval. The paper refers to Professor Sean Murphy's definition of humanitarian intervention as an accurate description of current understanding: the "threat or use of force by a state, group of states, or international organization primarily for the purpose of protecting the nationals of the target state from widespread deprivations of internationally recognized human rights." Id. p. 2. At: www.ploughshares.ca/libraries/WorkingPapers/wp012.html.

32. See the authorities cited in Ploughshares, supra, p. 6. Humanitarian interventions by regional organizations in Africa, both before and after NATO's action in Kosovo, could often be distinguished from the NATO action because the interventions were within the territory of Member States, who had agreed to the standards being enforced.

33. In Chapter IV.219, Secretary General Kofi Annan writes, "Surely no legal principle—not even sovereignty—can ever shield crimes against humanity. Where such crimes occur and peaceful attempts to halt them have been exhausted, the Security Council has a moral duty to act on behalf of the international community. The fact that we cannot protect people everywhere is no reason for doing nothing when we can. Armed intervention must always remain the option of last resort, but in the face of mass murder it is an option that cannot be relinquished." He goes on to say in Chapter VII.365 that a major priority of the United Nations and its members is "to strengthen respect for law, in international as in national affairs, in particular the agreed provisions of treaties on the control of armaments, and international humanitarian and human rights law." Kofi Annan, "We the Peoples: The Role of the UN in the 21st Century," April 3, 2000. Available at: www.un.org/millennium/sg/report/full.htm.

34. Chap. 6, Art. 24. "The Responsibility to Protect." Issued by the *International Commission on Intervention and State Sovereignty*, December 2001. Available at: www.iciss.ca/report2-en.asp.

35. Report at 66. The Report pointedly refers to this as a "responsibility to protect" and not a "right to intervene." Id. at 65.

36. An early advocate of this position was the late Lloyd Cutler, a leading U.S. lawyer and Counsel to two U.S. presidents. Cutler, Lloyd N., "The Right to Intervene," *Foreign Affairs* Vol. 64 No. 1 (1985). Other important advocates included Professors Lillich and Teson, and in re-

cent years the United Kingdom and Belgium have formally asserted the legality of humanitarian intervention to prevent catastrophes not otherwise preventable. See Gray, pp. 35–42.

37. See generally Coady, Tony & O'Keefe, Michael, eds., *Righteous Violence: The Ethics and Politics of Military Intervention* (Melbourne Univ. Press, Melbourne, Australia, 2005).

38. "It is further to be noted that, while Uganda claimed to have acted in self-defence, it did not ever claim that it had been subjected to an armed attack by the armed forces of the DRC. The 'armed attacks' to which reference was made came rather from the ADF. The Court has found above . . . that there is no satisfactory proof of the involvement in these attacks, direct or indirect, of the Government of the DRC. . . . The Court is of the view that, on the evidence before it, even if this series of deplorable attacks could be regarded as cumulative in character, they still remained non-attributable to the DRC." *Democratic Republic of the Congo v. Uganda*, Judgment, International Court of Justice, December 19, 2005, at para. 146.

39. See *Nicaragua v. United States of America*, Merits: Judgment, International Court of Justice, June 27, 1986, at paragraph 249: "On the legal level the Court cannot regard response to an intervention by Nicaragua as such a justification. While an armed attack would give rise to an entitlement to collective self-defence, a use of force of a lesser degree of gravity cannot. As the Court has already observed (paragraph 211 above) . . . The acts of which Nicaragua is accused, even assuming them to have been established and imputable to that State, could only have justified proportionate counter-measures on the part of the State which had been the victim of these acts, namely El Salvador, Honduras or Costa Rica. They could not justify counter-measures taken by a third State, the United States, and particularly could not justify intervention involving the use of force."

40. "UK Atty. Gen. Statement in the House of Lords," (April 21, 2004) at: www.publications.parliament.uk/pa/cm200304/canselect/cmfaff/441/4060808.htm. Christopher Greenwood has strongly supported this idea in "War, Terrorism, and International Law," supra, Chap. 4, n. 32, pp. 521–522.

41. Article 2(4) provides: "All Members shall refrain in their international relations from the threat or use of force against the territorial integrity or political independence of any state, or in any other manner

inconsistent with the Purposes of the United Nations." An excellent presentation of the position that the language of Article 2(4) was intended and should be read to prohibit only uses of force in violation of Charter purposes is D'Amato, Anthony, *International Law: Process and Prospect* (Transnational Publishers, Dobbs Ferry, N.Y., 1987), pp. 57–73.

42. Article 51 provides: "Nothing in the present Charter shall impair the inherent right of individual or collective self-defence if an armed attack occurs against a Member of the United Nations, until the Security Council has taken measures necessary to maintain international peace and security. Measures taken by Members in the exercise of this right of self-defence shall be immediately reported to the Security Council and shall not in any way affect the authority and responsibility of the Security Council under the present Charter to take at any time such action as it deems necessary in order to maintain or restore international peace and security." See Blum, Yehuda, "The Legality of State Response to Acts of Terrorism," in Netanyahu, Binyamin, ed., *Terrorism: How the West Can Win* (Farrar, Straus, Giroux, New York, 1986).

43. See generally Sofaer, Abraham D., "International Law and the Use of Force," *The National Interest*, no. 13 (Fall 1988) in Woolsey, R. James, *The National Interest: International Law & Order* (Transaction Publisher, New Brunswick, N.J., 2003), p. 45.

44. For example, when NATO Secretary General Xavier Solano wrote to the North Atlantic Council explaining the legitimacy of taking military action in Kosovo he cited the factors that supported the intervention: "[T]he Allies believe that in the particular circumstances with respect to the present crisis in Kosovo as described in UNSC Resolution 1199, there are legitimate grounds for the Alliance to threaten, and if necessary, to use force." Letter of Oct. 9, 1998, quoted in Bruno Simma, "NATO, The UN and the Use of Force: Legal Aspects: Kosovo: A Thin Red Line," 1999 *EJIL* 10(1). President Clinton handled the issue in the same manner. Statement to the Nation (24 March 1999) available at: www.whitehouse.gov/WH/New/html/19990324-2872.html.

45. Grotius, Hugo, *On the Law of War and Peace* (Kessinger Publishing, Whitefish, Mont., 2004), pp. 52–54: "[T]he first just cause of war, then, is an injury, which, even though not actually committed, threatens our persons or our property." Grotius goes on to say that "the danger must

be immediate, and, as it were, at the point of happening." The necessity of understanding a belligerent country's intentions became one of the key principles in legitimizing preventive or preemptive use of force, stating that "in order that defensive measures should be lawful, they must be necessary, as they are not unless we are certain not only of our neighbor's power but of his intentions." Later, Grotius makes the controversial statement that "a thing is said to be just, either through its cause, or because of its effects," implying that legitimacy can be ascribed to force either before or after its use. Stevens, supra, Chap. 1, n. 2, collects the views of Grotius, Puffendorf, and Vattel at pp. 103–104.

46. McDougal, Myres Smith & Feliciano, Florentino P., *The International Law of War: Transnational Coercion and World Public Order* (Martinus Nijhoff Publishers, Dordrecht, The Netherlands, 1994), pp. 218–220.

47. Hitler staged Operation Himmler on August 31, 1939, which included German soldiers who dressed as Polish soldiers and terrorized German customs posts, leaving behind murdered concentration camp victims dressed in Polish uniforms. The German soldiers also took over a Polish radio station, giving an anti-German speech in order to incite the German population. He used the acts to serve as justification to invade Poland on September 1, 1939. "Address by Adolf Hitler—September 1, 1939." Given before the Reichstag. At: www.yale.edu/lawweb/avalon/wwii/gp2.htm. Similarly, in what is known as the Mukden Incident, Japanese junior officers blew up a Japanese railroad in Manchuria. Japan blamed Chinese dissidents for the action, claimed self-defense, invaded Manchuria on September 19, 1931, and soon occupied Manchuria. "United States Relations with China: Boxer Uprising to Cold War (1900–1949)." Historical Background, Office of the Historian. At: www.state.gov/r/pa/ho/pubs/fs/90689.htm. Italy had been preparing for and attempting to gather support through the League of Nations to attack Ethiopia since 1932, with limited success. On December 5, 1934, a small border incident in the oasis of Wal Wal, Ethiopia, served as the pretext for Italy to attack Ethiopia on October 3, 1935, with Ethiopia coming under Italy's rule by 1936. Goodwin, Clayton, "When Italy Invaded Ethiopia . . . 70 years ago," *New African* (October 2005).

48. Henkin, Louis et al., *Right v. Might* (Council on Foreign Relations Press, New York, 1989), pp. 60–63.

49. The committee's full statement is notable and may reflect a widely held European view:

   "The 'new threats' cannot be classified as a more or less one-dimensional problem, unlike the situations that call for humanitarian intervention (i.e., massive violations of fundamental human rights for which the only solution would appear to be the use of force and about which there is widespread consensus). Instead, the 'new threats' and their breeding grounds can take on all sorts of conceivable forms (and perhaps even forms that cannot yet be conceived) that do not lend themselves to prior definition and for which there are no ready-made solutions. Any attempt to do so would lead either to extreme detail or to excessive vagueness. In both cases, there is a great risk of giving an unintended impression of legitimating such military action in advance."

   Report, supra note 7, p. 31.

50. The balance of consequences element is analogous to the requirement of "just war" theory that any action should do less harm than good. This should require evaluations of uses of force to be made in the context of a comprehensive judgment based on all relevant political factors, not merely the capacity to carry off the strike without major collateral consequences. Walzer, Michael, *Just and Unjust Wars* (Basic Books, New York, 1997), pp. 127–37.

51. Goldsmith, Jack & Posner, Eric, *The Limits of International Law* (Oxford Univ. Press, New York, 2006). Bork, Robert H., "The Limits of 'International Law'," *The National Interest*, no. 18 (Winter 1989/90) in Woolsey, James R., *The National Interest: International Law and Order* (Transaction Publishers, New Brunswick, N.J., 2003) pp. 43–45. This position differs from that of Ambassador Jeane Kirkpatrick, and others, that on the basis of reciprocity States should not be bound to abide by use-of-force limitations in responding to the actions of other States that disregard those rules. Kirkpatrick, Jeane, "Law and Reciprocity," 1986 *A.S.I.L* 59.

52. Those who support this position argue, essentially, that it was the intended arrangement under the Charter and should be accepted, presumably unless it is changed through amendment. For example, former ICJ President Bohdan Winiarski stated: "The intention of those who drafted it was clearly to abandon the possibility of useful action

rather than to sacrifice the balance of carefully established fields of competence, as can be seen, for example, in the case of the voting in the Security Council. It is only by such procedures, which were clearly defined, that the United Nations can seek to achieve its purposes. It may be that the United Nations is sometimes not in a position to undertake action which would be useful for the maintenance of international peace and security or for one or another of the purposes indicated in Article 1 of the Charter, but that is the way in which the Organization was conceived and brought into being." Quoted in Laursen, Andreas, "The Use of Force and (the State of) Necessity," 37 *Vand. J. Transnat'l L.* 485 (2004).

Chapter 7

1. "Humanitarian Intervention: Legal and Political Aspects" 103 (1999) (prepared by the Danish Institute for Foreign Affairs for the Foreign Minister).
2. See Weisburd, pp. 1–27.
3. On May 22, 2003, the Security Council passed Resolution 1483 transferring Iraq's oil revenue to the Development Fund for Iraq, with the finances controlled by the Coalition Provisional Authority. Maintaining coalition control in Iraq was widely condemned, even by States normally aligned with the U.S. The *New York Times* reported that the U.S. chose not to hand over coalition control to the UN in exchange for peacekeepers from countries such as France and India. "After the War: The Occupation; U.S. Abandons Idea of Bigger UN Role in Iraq Occupation," *New York Times*, August 14, 2003, available at: www.nytimes.com/2003/08/14/world/after-war-occupation-us-abandons-idea-bigger-un-role-iraq-occupation.html?scp=7&sq=2003%20occupation%20france%20iraq&st=cse.
4. E.g., Murphy, Sean D., *Humanitarian Intervention: The United Nations in an Evolving World Order* (Univ. Pa. Press, 1996), p. 384: "developing criteria might serve less to restrain unilateral humanitarian intervention and more to provide a pretext for abusive intervention." See, Roberts, Adam, "NATO's 'Humanitarian War' over Kosovo," *Survival* 41(3), pp. 102–03: "most states . . . are nervous about justifying in advance a type of operation which might further increase the power of major powers, and might be used against them; and . . . NATO

members and other states are uneasy about creating a doctrine which might oblige them to intervene" when they do not want to do so.

5. Among the most valuable are Simons, Penelope C., "Humanitarian Intervention: A Review of Literature," Ploughshares Working Paper 01–2, pp. 17–18, (Ploughshares); Doyle, Michael W., *Striking First: Preemption and Prevention in International Conflict* (Princeton Univ. Press, Princeton, N.J., 2008), pp. 9–10, 57–59. See also Walzer, Michael, *Just and Unjust Wars* (Basic Books, New York, 1977), pp. 61–63 (discussing the legalist paradigm).

6. The Danish Institute for Foreign Affairs Report on humanitarian intervention proposes: "the definition of violations which may justify humanitarian intervention should be narrow in order to avoid abuse and to establish clearly its moral and political legitimacy." Report 106.

7. Abview, Francis Kofi, *The Evolution of the Doctrine and Practice of Humanitarian Intervention* (Kluwer Law International, The Hague, Netherlands, 1998), p. 271.

8. "All peaceful avenues which may be explored consistent with the urgency of the situation to achieve a solution based on negotiation, discussion and any other means short of force have been exhausted, notwithstanding which, no solution can be agreed upon by the parties to the conflict." Cassese, Antonio, "Ex iniura ius oritur: Are We Moving towards International Legitimation of Forcible Humanitarian Countermeasures in the World Community?" 1999 *EJIL* 10(23).

9. The fact that the NPT has built-in discrimination between nuclear and non-nuclear weapon States would need to be taken into account if greater restrictions on non-nuclear States are to be developed, potentially with greater reliance on benefits for such States to go along with new restrictions or enhanced enforcement.

10. A particularly helpful analysis is Franck, Thomas M., "On Proportionality of Countermeasures in International Law," 102 A.J.I.L. 715 (2008).

11. Maogoto, p. 95.

12. Protocol Additional to the Geneva Conventions on the Law of War of 1949, and relating to the Protection of Victims of International Armed Conflicts (Protocol 1). Available at: www.unhchr.ch/html/menu3/b/93.htm. The U.S. has not ratified Protocol 1, but recognizes

that its limits on the use of force during armed conflict reflect customary international law.

13. "Military and Paramilitary Activities in and against Nicaragua" (*Nicaragua v. United States of America*), Merits: Judgment, International Court of Justice (27 June 1986), para. 176. The Court concluded: "self-defense would warrant only measures which are proportional to the armed attack and necessary to respond to it, a rule well established in customary international law."

14. For example in summarizing the U.S. position on defeating terrorism and preventing attacks on the U.S. and its friends and allies, the 2006NSS states (p. 8): "To succeed in our own efforts, we need the support and concerted action of friends and allies."

15. Danish Report, supra at 108.

16. Ploughshares, p. 19.

17. The 2006NSS notes (p. 19) the passage of UN Security Council Resolution 1540 in April 2004 requiring nations to criminalize WMD proliferation and institute effective export and financial controls.

18. The 2006NSS (p. 17) concludes: "genocide must not be tolerated." It makes no similar commitment concerning torture, although the U.S. and most other States have made torture and other cruel, inhuman, and degrading treatment universally illegal and subject to criminal prosecution under national laws.

19. Despite its emphasis on the spread of freedom and democracy as being fundamental to U.S. security, the 2006NSS states (p. 5) "freedom cannot be imposed; it must be chosen." Some support exists, however, for the proposition that U.N. Charter purposes include a preference for political freedom for all peoples, and particularly for the right of a democratically elected government to continue in office until it is lawfully replaced. Wheatley, Steven, "The Security Council, Democratic Legitimacy and Regime Change in Iraq," 2006 *EJIL* 17 (531). A useful discussion of this issue is in Gray, pp. 42–44.

20. Levitt, Jeremy I., "Pro-Democratic Intervention in Africa," 24 *Wis. Int'l L.J.* 785 (2006).

21. The Statute of the International Court of Justice, Article 38, states that "the Court, whose function is to decide in accordance with international law such disputes as are submitted to it, shall apply: the general principles of law recognized by civilized nations" (Art. 38, 1(c)).

22. Ploughshares, p. 19.

23. Id., pp. 19–20.

24. Cassese, Antonio, "Ex iniura ius oritur: Are We Moving towards International Legitimation of Forcible Humanitarian Countermeasures in the World Community?" 1999 *EJIL* 10(23).

25. Ploughshares, p. 21.

26. Koh, Harold Hongju, "Comment," Doyle, Michael W., *Striking First: Preemption and Prevention in International Conflict* (Princeton Univ. Press, Princeton, N.J., 2008), pp. 115–116.

27. Jonathan Charney argues that evidence of grave crimes must be publicly available to justify a humanitarian intervention. "Anticipatory Humanitarian Intervention in Kosovo," 32 *Vand. J. of Transnat'l Law* 1231 (1999). Evidence of humanitarian threats is more likely to be publicly available than of most other forms of threats.

28. National Commission on Terrorist Attacks Upon the United States (2004); Commission on the Intelligence Capabilities of the United States Regarding Weapons of Mass Destruction (2005). The 2006NSS notes the findings of the Iraq Survey Group and the two commissions and cites (pp. 23–24) as a major improvement the creation of a "single, accountable leader of the intelligence community with authorities to match his responsibilities, and increased sharing of information and increased resources . . . ." The Director of National Intelligence is now responsible for improved collection and evaluation of intelligence.

29. The High-level Panel report includes a number of proposals to enhance the Security Council's capacities to deal with threats. It recognizes that one reason States may want to bypass the Council "is a lack of confidence in the quality and objectivity of its decision-making. The Council's decisions have often been less than consistent, less than persuasive and less than fully responsive to very real State and human security needs. But," the Report concludes, "the solution is not to reduce the Council to impotence and irrelevance: it is to work from within to reform it . . . " Report at 64.

30. Charney, Jonathan, I., "NATO's Kosovo Intervention: Anticipatory Humanitarian Intervention in Kosovo," 93 *A.J.I.L.* 834 (1999).

31. The ICJ construed the U.S./Nicaragua Friendship Commerce and Navigation Treaty to confer authority on the Court to determine whether the U.S. had used illegal force against Nicaragua.

32. "Elements of Crimes," International Criminal Court: Assembly of Parties, entry into force September 9, 2002. Available at: www.icc-cpi.int/NR/rdonlyres/9CAEE830-38CF-41D6-AB0B-68E5F9082543/0/Element_of_Crimes_English.pdf.

33. "Court Looks at Supporters of Rebels in Colombia," *New York Times*, August 16, 2008, at: www.nytimes.com/2008/08/16/world/americas/16colombia.html?_r=1&scp=1&sq=%E2%80%9CCourt%20Looks%20At%20Supporters%20of%20Rebels%20in%20Colombia%E2%80%9D%20&st=cse.

34. Statement of Secretary of Defense Robert M. Gates to the Senate Appropriations Committee-Defense, May 20, 2008. Available at: http://appropriations.senate.gov/Hearings/2008_05_20_-Defense-_Testimony_of_Defense_Secretary_Gates_at_May_20th_Defense_Subcommittee_Hearing.pdf?CFID=6834464&CFTOKEN=4035094.

35. "Gates Tries to Ease Tension in Afghan Civilian Deaths," by Thom Shanker, *New York Times*, September 17, 2008, at www.nytimes.com/2008/09/18/world/asia/18gates.html?_r=1&scp=1&sq=&st.

36. E.g., "Five Killed in Mideast Clashes. Israel Issues Apology for Civilian Casualties," *Boston Globe*, September 2, 2002.

About the Author

*A*braham D. Sofaer was appointed the first George P. Shultz Distinguished Scholar and senior fellow at the Hoover Institution in 1994. Having served as legal adviser to the U.S. Department of State from 1985 to 1990, his work focuses on separation of powers issues in the American system of government, including the power over war, and on issues related to international law, terrorism, diplomacy, national security, and the Middle East conflict. He was a principal negotiator in various interstate matters that were successfully resolved, including the dispute between Egypt and Israel over Taba, the claim against Iraq for its attack on the USS *Stark*, and the claims against Chile for the assassination of diplomat Orlando Letelier. He received the Distinguished Service Award in 1989, the highest state department award given to a non–civil servant.

Sofaer was a clerk to Judge J. Skelly Wright on the U.S. Court of Appeals in Washington, D.C., and to the Honorable William J. Brennan Jr., associate justice of the U.S. Supreme Court from 1965 to 1967. From 1967 to 1969, Sofaer was an assistant U.S. attorney in the Southern District of New York; from 1969 to 1979, he was a professor of law at Columbia University School of Law, during which time he wrote *War, Foreign Affairs, and Constitutional Power*, an account of the constitutional powers of Congress and the president to control or affect the use of force. In 1979, Sofaer was appointed a U.S. district judge in the Southern District of New York, where he served until 1985. A veteran of the U.S. Air Force, Sofaer received an LLB degree from New York University School of Law in 1965, where he was editor in chief of the law review.

The Stanford Task Force on Preventive Force

ASSOCIATE MEMBERS

William Burke-White
United States Department of State
Office of Foreign Policy Planning

Anne-Marie Slaughter
Director of Policy Planning
United States Department of State

Stephen E. Miller
Director of the International Security
  Program
Belfer Center of Science & International
  Affairs
Harvard University

STAFF

James E. Fannell
National Security Affairs Fellow
Hoover Institution

Catharine Kristian
Executive Assistant to Coit Blacker

Megan Reiss
Research Associate

Grace Goldberger
Executive Assistant to Abraham Sofaer

Dennis Mandudzo
Research Associate

Scott Tait
National Security Affairs Fellow
Hoover Institution

Matt Weingart
National Security Affairs Fellow
Hoover Institution

Index